SOCIOLOGY IN FOCUS SERIES
General Editor: Murray Morison

The Sociology of Development

Graham Harris M.A.,
Senior Lecturer,
East Warwickshire College

LONGMAN
London and New York

Longman Group UK Limited,
Longman House, Burnt Mill, Harlow,
Essex CM20 2JE, England
and Associated Companies throughout the world.

Published in the United States of America
by Longman Inc., New York.

First published 1989
Third impression 1993

Set in 10/11point Bembo, Linotron 202
Printed in Malaysia by TCP

ISBN 0 582 35563X

The publisher's policy is to use paper
manufactured from sustainable forests.

British Library Cataloguing in Publication Data
 Harris Graham
 The sociology of development. – (Sociology in focus
 series)
 1. Developing countries. Cultural processes, –
 Sociological perspectives
 I. Title II. Series
 306'.09172'4

 ISBN 0-582-35563-X

Library of Congress Cataloging-in-Publication Data
Harris, Graham.
 The sociology of development/Graham Harris.
  p.   cm. – (Sociology in focus series)
 Bibliography: p.
 Includes index.
 ISBN 0-582-35563-X
 1. Economic development – Sociological aspects. I. Title.
II. Series.
HD75.H34 1989
306.3 – dc20

89-2697
CIP

Contents

Acknowledgements

I would like to thank Mary Maynard of York University for reading the manuscript and providing helpful advice and suggestions. I must also thank the series editor, Murray Morison, for his support and encouragement throughout the venture.

I am grateful to Pat Sear of East Warwickshire College for her help in dealing with an often capricious word processor and Bettina Wilkes, the copyeditor, for her help in untangling grammatical convolutions. I am also grateful to Felicity Peadon and Judith Orrill of the College Library and to the staff of the *Guardian* Library for their help in finding source material.

Special thanks go to my wife, Linda, for her forebearance and her help in the preparation of the index.

We are grateful to the following for permission to reproduce tables and diagrams: *Population & Development*, Macmillan Education, 1986, Figure 9.1; J. Petras and R. Rhodes, *New Left Review*, May–June 1974, Figure 6.1; *Human Numbers, Human Needs*, International Planned Parenthood Federation, Figure 10.1; cartoon entitled 'Suffering' by Posy Simmonds, reprinted by permission of the Peters Fraser & Dunlop Group Ltd; Kaye & Ward, *Population Today*, Octopus Publishing Group plc, Figures 9.5, tables (p. 89), table (p. 98).

We are grateful to the following for permission to reproduce copyright material: Philip Allan Publishers Ltd for an extract from the article 'Explaining Africa's Famine' by R. Bush in *Social Studies Review* Vol. 2 No. 3 (January 1987); The Associated Examining Board for questions from past examination papers; Bogle L'Ouverture Publications Ltd, Howard University Press and Tanzania Publishing for extracts from *How Europe Underdeveloped Africa* by Walter Rodney; Cambridge University Press for extracts from *The Stages of Economic Growth* by W. W. Rostow (19th Edition, November 1969) and an extract from *The Sociology of the Third World* by J. G. Goldthorpe (1979); EMI Music Publishing Ltd, International Music Publications & Warner Chappell, Inc for an extract from the song 'Is This The World We Created' by F Mercury & B May, © 1984 Queen Music Ltd; University of London School Examinations Board for a question from a past examination paper; Monthly Review Foundation for extracts from *Latin America: Underdevelopment or Revolution* by A. G. Frank, copyright © 1970 by Andre Gunder Frank; Unwin Hyman Ltd for an extract from *Class Structure and Economic Growth* by A Maddison (George Allen & Unwin Ltd, 1971).

We have been unable to trace the copyright holder in *Population Today* by Eric McGraw (Kaye & Ward, 1979) and would appreciate any information that would enable us to do so.

Series introduction

Sociology in Focus aims to provide an up-to-date, coherent coverage of the main topics that arise on an introductory course in sociology. While the intention is to do justice to the intricacy and complexity of current issues in sociology, the style of writing has deliberately been kept simple. This is to ensure that the student coming to these ideas for the first time need not become lost in what can appear initially as jargon.

Each book in the series is designed to show something of the purpose of sociology and the craft of the sociologist. Throughout the different topic areas the interplay of theory, methodology and social policy have been highlighted, so that rather than sociology appearing as an unwieldy collection of facts, the student will be able to grasp something of the process whereby sociological understanding is developed. The format of the books is broadly the same throughout. Part 1 provides an overview of the topic as a whole. In Part 2 the relevant research is set in the context of the theoretical, methodological and policy issues. The student is encouraged to make his or her own assessment of the various arguments, drawing on the statistical and reference material provided both here and at the end of the book. The final part of the book contains both statistical material and a number of 'Readings'. Questions have been provided in this section to direct students to analyse the materials presented in terms of both theoretical assumptions and methodological approaches. It is intended that this format should enable students to exercise their own sociological imaginations rather than to see sociology as a collection of universally accepted facts, which just have to be learned.

While each book in the series is complete within itself, the similarity of format ensures that the series as a whole provides an integrated and balanced introduction to sociology. It is intended that the text can be used both for individual and classroom study while the inclusion of the varied statistical and documentary materials lend themselves to both the preparation of essays and brief seminars.

Is this the world we created . . .? (Mercury/May)

Just think of all those hungry mouths we have to feed
Take a look at all the suffering we breed
So many lonely faces scattered all around
Searching for what they need.

Is this the world we created
What did we do it for
Is this the world we invaded
Against the law
So it seems in the end
Is this what we're all living for today
The world we created.

You know that everyday a helpless child is born
Who needs some loving care inside a happy home
Somewhere a wealthy man is sitting on his throne
Waiting for life to go by.

Is this the world we created, we made it on our own
Is this the world we devastated, right to the bone
If there's a God in the sky looking down
What can he think of what we've done
To the world that he created.

Queen Music Ltd/EMI Music Publishing Ltd

For unto every one that hath shall be given, and he shall have abun-
dance; but from him that hath not shall be taken away even that which
he hath.

(Matt. 25:29)

Dedication

To the memory of my mother, Doris Harris

PART 1

Developmentalist/modernisation theory

1 Development: themes and issues

From time to time our televisions and newspapers show harrowing pictures and give graphic accounts of the appalling plight of people in the many areas of famine around the world. Stories such as these help to focus public attention on starvation and disease which is the life experience for so many of our fellow human beings. Perhaps the most common reaction is that of pity, and, frequently, private consciences stir public actions, which result in large sums of money being collected in order to buy food and medicines for the starving.

Occasionally, too, anger and frustration are expressed by some of those involved in trying to alleviate the suffering of these people. There is anger at the ludicrous spectacle of surplus food being held in expensive stockpiles throughout the affluent nations. Frustration is felt because, in spite of apparently endless discussion amongst politicians with many mouthings of good intent, nothing substantial ever seems to be done. 'Third World' (see Figure 1.1) famine and poverty is, sadly, a recurrent theme, and world leaders seem either unable or unwilling to resolve the tragic paradox of millions starving in a world where excess food is stockpiled or destroyed.

Simply to concentrate upon the extremes of famine, however, important as this is, is to misrepresent the world situation. The nations of the world, like the individuals within each nation, exist in a hierarchy of affluence which ranges from utter destitution to immense wealth. Generally, the most affluent nations are to be found in the northern hemisphere and the poorer nations in the southern hemisphere of the earth (see Figure 1.2). It is when we ask why it is and how it is that, in spite of all the noble rhetoric

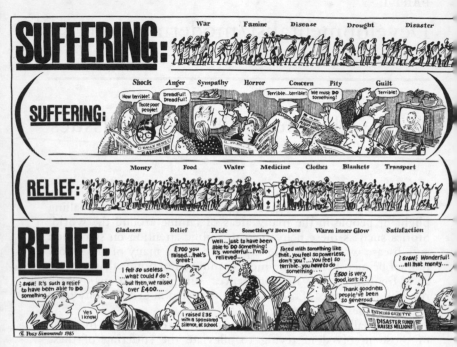

Source: the Guardian, 28 January 1985

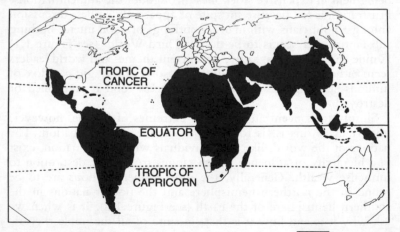

Figure 1.1 The Third World

 Third World

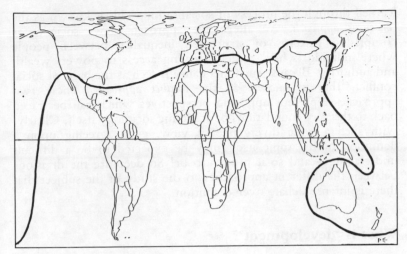

Figure 1.2   'North' and 'South'

from politicians and the immense good will of ordinary people, the disadvantaged remain so vastly impoverished that we approach the subject of social development from a sociological perspective.

Sociologists are concerned with the analysis of economic and social differences among people both within nations and among nations, and to suggest reasons for these differentials. Why, after so many generations, have those people who Fanon has called 'the wretched of the earth' not even begun to achieve a standard of living equal to that of those in the wealthy nations? Indeed, we may wish to go further and ask why there is such a vast discrepancy between nations at all, either in terms of wealth or the quality of life of their citizens. Is there a sort of 'Holy Grail' of development, the possession of which enables hunger, disease and homelessness to be eradicated? It is with questions such as these that the study of social development is concerned, and, in this introductory volume, we shall try to examine the main themes and issues involved in its sociological analysis.

The task is not an easy one, however, because the study of development exposes fundamental theoretical divisions within sociology. One theoretical approach views societies as essentially harmonious units in which people conform to a system of values learned through the process of socialisation. This is known as the *consensus approach*. An alternative approach views societies as comprising patterns of structured inequality between people where individuals have widely varying access to power, wealth and authority. Because such inequality is seen as the basis of social conflict, this is known as the *conflict approach*. These two approaches represent opposing perspectives which can be traced back to the very foundations of academic sociology itself. Clearly, with such a wide divergence of view, even agreeing upon a definition of the topic itself may be expected to be a difficult undertaking – and so it proves to be! So deep are the divisions between the different approaches to the study of the subject that there is intense debate over definition.

What is 'development'?

At some time in the past (estimates range from 10 000 to 20 000 years ago) our ancestors lived in primitive 'hunter–gatherer' societies in which the problems of survival were resolved by communal effort. The edible parts of wild vegetation and small animals, insects and grubs were collected and eaten. Other groups perhaps hunted larger animals which also provided food while, in addition, their skins provided material for clothing and their bones could be made into useful implements. The life style of these, our early ancestors, implied that they existed in a fragile relationship with the forces of nature. In consequence, it is fairly easy to see why they were a mystical people who, from archaeological evidence, constantly tried to appease the 'gods' of sun, earth and rain. It has been estimated that each person in such a hunter–gatherer system would need over 2 square miles of land in order to survive. This meant that the people were forced to follow a nomadic existence, constantly searching for the essentials of life.

From these beginnings human beings in society have gradually gained increased control over the forces of nature. There is, however, widespread variation in the degree to which this has happened. Some societies have advanced far in this respect and have taken on an urban, industrial character; others have remained largely agrarian in character, and still exist very much at the mercy of the forces of nature.

A number of theories have been advanced to try and explain why these changes came about, and why they occurred at such widely differing rates in different parts of the world. A useful background against which to examine some of the main theories is to trace the pattern of changes which modern urban, industrial societies underwent in the process of acquiring their present form of social organisation.

Three clearly identifiable periods in the history of industrial societies may be seen as the 'bench-marks' of social change. In other words, they may be said to represent the points at which major changes in social and economic organisation have taken place. These phases may be called:

1 the Agrarian Revolution;
2 the Commercial Revolution;
3 the Industrial Revolution.

Each of these will now be examined briefly in turn.

The Agrarian Revolution

The early hunter–gatherer societies were nomadic, because the people were obliged constantly to widen their search for the meagre sources of food upon which they depended. Gradually, after many generations, groups began to settle in the more fertile areas where they could grow the food for which they had previously foraged. In these settlements they also began taming and domesticating animals for use both as food and as beasts of burden. This, together with the planned cultivation of food, resulted in life becoming generally rather less uncertain, and gradually the overall standard of life improved.

All this brought about conditions of greater social stability which, though still very precarious by the standards of modern industrial societies, led to a small but consistent increase in the quality of life. More people could be supported from the land because of the increased availability of food, although it must be noted that this was still an era of subsistence-level existence with a high birth rate accompanied by an extremely high infant mortality rate and a low expectation of life. In short, conditions were very harsh indeed.

As agriculture took hold and flourished, so *land* grew in importance and hence in value as it became a commodity in its own right. Land was a valuable resource which could, with advances in agricultural production technique, be cultivated for profit. As a result, people became either the *owners* or *non-owners* of land; societies became internally stratified, using as a criterion for group membership the relationship of each individual to land. The landowning *stratum* (layer) became the aristocracy, while the large mass of non-landowners became a subservient peasant stratum, a situation which formed the basis of the *estate system* in *feudal society*. In addition, the landowning minority held political and military power while the landless peasants provided the labour power under conditions of virtual slavery.

In the fifteenth and sixteenth centuries European explorers and adventurers made perilous voyages to far-off lands – a spirit of adventure and a search for knowledge which was matched in other areas of endeavour. In science, for example, new approaches to the study of the physical world led to major discoveries and heralded what has been termed the 'Age of Reason'; a period in which rational analysis and precision of measurement under experimental conditions began to replace earlier superstition and mysticism.

The seventeenth and eighteenth centuries yielded improvements in communication techniques with the advent of printing and the development of transport. This was a period of accelerating innovation within Europe where ideas generated enterprise and promoted new forms of economic and social organisation. Merchants and entrepreneurs (promoters of commercial deals), keen to expand their businesses and to increase their wealth, were quick to recognise the potential of trading with nations overseas, with the result that, having long ago changed from a nomadic to a settled life style, the Europeans once again became travellers. This time, however, there was a significant change in that travel was no longer a question of subsistence but of survival in another 'jungle' – that of business and the pursuit of profit in the market: the era of commercial trading had arrived.

The Commercial Revolution

It is hardly an exaggeration to claim that this period resulted in the total transformation of the systems of production, distribution and exchange throughout Europe and, ultimately, far beyond. From a small–scale, mainly domestic, pattern of production and trading among the towns and villages of European nations, there emerged a large-scale commercial trading network which was international in character. The seventeenth and eighteenth centuries saw trade expand among the countries of Europe and the conquest of the continent of Africa. The exploration and subsequent colonisation of South America, together with the opening up of the great trading routes to the Far East and the Indies, provided great opportunities for commercial enterprise amongst those European merchants of adventurous spirit. Businesses flourished as the demand for the produce and resources of exotic lands grew quickly in Europe. In consequence, large quantities of silks, spices, gold, silver and slaves were imported into Europe, gaining great riches for the merchants involved in their trade.

In Britain, the Bank of England (founded in 1694) integrated and enlarged the banking system into a more coherent economic and social institution. Joint stock companies developed, which, together with facilities for the lending of capital, enabled new trading and commercial ventures to be financed. The joint stock companies enabled large amounts of capital to be raised because, by holding a variety of shares in a range of different enterprises, investors saw that their risks were considerably reduced and so were encouraged to invest.

The great expansion in the size and complexity of commercial enterprise during this period brought with it corresponding changes in social attitudes. A new approach to economic and social relations developed which underpinned the making of profit. This approach was typified by a social climate which was 'individualistic, competitive . . . and offering opportunities for speculative gain on a scale unknown before' (R. H. Tawney, *Religion and the Rise of Capitalism*, Pelican, 1940, p. 85). These new acquisitive attitudes were strengthened by the decline of Catholicism over significant parts of Western Europe. In its place people were turning to Protestantism – or, more especially, Calvinism – a creed which emphasises labour as a form of religious worship. By virtue of hard work a person was expected to praise God while, at the same time, refraining from the sinful pursuit of frivolous enjoyment of the fruit of that labour. This 'Protestant Ethic', as Max Weber called it, was 'bound directly to influence the development of a capitalistic way of life' (M. Weber, *The Protestant Ethic and the Spirit of Capitalism*, Unwin, 1971, p. 166). God was duly praised and glorified by the faithful, with the result that large capital reserves were built up and, through being invested in new economic enterprises, they provided the foundation of capitalist industry and commerce.

At the same time the population of Europe was growing, due to improvements in overall standards of living. Indeed, European societies were about to enter a period of remarkable inventiveness which was to be truly revolutionary in its effect. There developed a situation, at first in Britain but soon throughout Europe, which David Landes has termed 'critical mass' (D. Landes, *Technological Change and Development in Western Europe, 1750–1914, The Cambridge Economic History of Europe*, vol. VI, CUP, 1965, p. 277). This was a condition in which all the ingredients necessary for the transformation of the economic system appeared simultaneously. Amongst these ingredients may be included: capital, technological innovation, labour power and raw materials, together with entrepreneurial spirit and a market which could be reached by an efficient transport network. Such a list is not, of course, to be seen as exhaustive, but the important thing to note is that the resulting 'explosion' of economic activity set in motion that series of momentous events known collectively as 'the Industrial Revolution'. This constitutes what is sometimes described as 'the great divide', that chasm

> between a world of slow economic growth in which populations and real incomes were increasing slowly or not at all, and a world of much faster economic growth, in which population has increased at an almost frightening rate and in which there has been sustained increases in real income per head.
> (R. M. Hartwell, *The Causes of the Industrial Revolution in England*, Methuen, 1972, p. 1)

The Industrial Revolution

Precisely when the Industrial Revolution 'began' is a matter for dispute amongst historians. In general terms, the change to industrial methods of production may be seen from the early parts of the eighteenth century onwards in Britain. The term 'revolution' is therefore misleading because it implies a process of rapid change when, in fact, the processes involved occurred over many years – if not generations! The significant point for our purposes is, however, that this was a time of great technological innovation which transformed the entire economic and social fabric of the nation. Small-scale agrarian communities, whose economy centred on subsistence food production supplemented perhaps by cottage industries such as weaving, were gradually replaced by large-scale factory production systems.

The decline in the demand for labour in agriculture and the corresponding increase in the demand for labour in the new factories resulted in the rapid growth of towns and cities – a process known as *urbanisation*. In the towns and cities, people could work for wages instead of produce, as previously in the villages. This shift of emphasis from the land to the industrial system as a prime economic factor resulted in the emergence of a new social group; the bourgeoisie, comprising capitalists and the professional middle class. This group, together with a new form of industrial 'working class' – the proletariat, propertyless wage-earners who exist by selling their labour power – formed the new equation of industrial production. The bourgeoisie largely replaced the feudal lords as predominant in the economic hierarchy (though not, it must be stressed, in the social or political hierarchy), while the proletariat approximated to the landless peasants of the feudal era.

A principal feature of the industrial system of production has always been the efficient mass production, at low cost, of usable commodities. The division of labour – a process by which occupational roles and tasks in society are allocated in an ideologically legitimated way – within the factory system ensured that a product of great complexity involving many different parts could be assembled rapidly and efficiently. Large-batch production together with the bulk purchase of raw materials and the low wages paid to workers ensured that high profits were made by the capitalist class.

Soon industrial Britain became known as 'the workshop of the world', and vast fortunes were made from the rapid growth in the domestic and overseas markets for mass-produced, low-priced goods. Mass production ensured the importance of the industrial system and, without doubt, improved the overall living standards of many millions. No longer was an individual required simply to endure the rigours of subsistence-level production, for the ripest fruits of new technology were available to be consumed – at a price. The supply of the goods and the services resulting from the industrial mass production were rationed in accordance with 'market forces'; that is, the ability of the individual to pay for them. Thus the engine of capitalism was fired, for, as the Hammonds observed: 'Mass production demands popular consumption . . . the command of a wide market is essential to the organisation of large-scale industry' (J. L. Hammond and B. Hammond, *The Rise of Modern Industry*, Methuen, 1947, pp. viii–67). In short, the industrial process may be said to have brought about a

> social system characteristic of our modern civilisation, which forms a whole as complete and as coherent as the feudal system of the tenth century can have been. But whilst the latter was the consequence of military necessity and of the dangers which threatened human life in a Europe given over to anarchical barbarism, the former has been produced by a concatenation of purely economic factors, grouped round the central fact of the factory system.
>
> (P. Mantoux, *The Industrial Revolution in the Eighteenth Century*, Methuen, 1966, p. 27)

Is industrialisation development? – the convergence thesis

In the majority of the more affluent nations an industrial system of production has grown and flourished. Not all industrial societies have followed the same political pathway, however. The capitalist industrial system, in which the ownership of the means of production, distribution and exchange is restricted to a minority of the population, spread out across Western Europe to North America and many other parts of the world. In contrast, there are other societies in which industrialisation has occurred without the use of privately-owned capital; for example, in the Soviet Union, China and the 'Eastern bloc' countries.

Because of this difference of approach industrial nations may conveniently be grouped according to the political system governing their economic relations; those, mainly Western, industrial nations which follow a capitalist system (First World nations) and those, mainly Eastern, industrial nations which follow a state-ownership system (Second World nations). In both of these 'worlds' the overall result may be said to be broadly similar, in that the affluence generated by the industrial system sets them apart from the poorer nations of the southern hemisphere (Third World nations); see Figure 1.1.

The 'wind of change' which began to blow through international relations after the end of the Second World War signalled the end of direct imperialist rule and the emergence of a new order in which old empires gave way to newly independent nation-states. Theoretically, these nations held sovereignty over their own destiny, and they developed a collective identity as the 'Third World' following a conference of twenty-nine Asian and African countries held in Bandung, Indonesia, during 1955. Despite the fact that some of the participating nations were, at the time of the conference, still formally colonies, the leaders were unanimous in asserting their right to a voice in world affairs. By making this declaration the Third World leaders changed perceptions not only of themselves but also those of the affluent industrial nations. These changed perceptions were to have far-reaching consequences, since they altered for ever the terms upon which the conduct of international relations was to be based. There grew a theoretical and ideological vision of the impoverished nations which Nigel Harris has called 'Third Worldism' (Nigel Harris, *The End of the Third World*, Penguin, 1987, p. 11). What this vision involved was the pursuit of answers to fundamental questions about the nature and causes of international affluence and poverty, and it gave rise to a highly specialised sector of economic analysis known as 'development economics'.

Some theorists have indicated that the process of industrialisation in itself brings about similar patterns of social organisation in all societies which experience it, irrespective of the political philosophy which underlies the economy. This view is known as the *convergence thesis*, and it represents the views of those theorists who claim that both capitalist and communist industrial societies ultimately develop along similar organisational lines. This implies that the 'pyramid' shape of traditional society would be superseded by a diamond- or elliptical-shaped social formation with the majority of the population in the middle range. This majority would be mainly involved in *tertiary* (service) *industries* rather than in *primary* (extractive) or *secondary* (manufacturing) *industries*.

Clark Kerr states the convergence theorist case as follows:

The place the society starts from and the route it follows are likely to affect its industrial features for many years, but all industrialising societies respond to the inherent logic of industrialism itself. The empire of industrialism will embrace the whole world; and such similarities as it decrees will penetrate the outermost points of its sphere of influence, and its sphere comes to be universal.

(C. Kerr, J. Dunlop, F. Harbison and C. Myers, *Industrialism and Industrial Man*, Heinemann, 1962, p. 46)

One perspective on developmental analysis therefore has, as its base, a belief that it is the process of industrialisation which provides the material affluence necessary to bring about the process of development. Such a view is known as the '*developmentalist*', or '*modernisation*', approach, and holds that it is necessary for societies to be changed from simple, traditional forms to complex, modern forms of economic, social and cultural systems (see T. Parsons, *The Social System*, Free Press, 1951; W. W. Rostow, *The Stages of Economic Growth*, CUP, 1969; S. N. Eisenstadt, *Tradition, Change and Modernity*, Wiley, 1973; A. Inkeles, *Exploring Individual Modernity*, Columbia University Press, 1983). A fundamental component of this body of theory is the assumption that a spirit of enterprise amongst the population will bring about conditions necessary for a 'take-off into growth' (Rostow, 1969; M. Olson, *The Rise and Decline of Nations: Economic Growth, Stagflation and Social Rigidities*, Yale University Press, 1982; E. Gilder, *The Spirit of Enterprise*, Simon & Schuster, 1984).

Chapters 2, 3 and 4 of this book will examine this theoretical position, both in terms of its own emergence as a body of analysis, and also critically in order to provide a background for the second part of the book, which follows the changing dimensions of analysis from aspects *internal* to a specific society towards the study of relations *between* societies.

The analysis of conditions in the Third World relative to the developed world has shown graphically that forecasts made by developmentalist theoreticians and ideologues have not been achieved. In response to this apparent theoretical inadequacy another analytical perspective – *dependency theory* – emerged, which has pointed to the system of economic relations between the developed and the underdeveloped Third World nations. From this perspective it is the global economic system which, at best, is seen to inhibit Third World development; at worst, it is seen as the main cause of underdevelopment and widespread poverty. Dependency theorists owe much to the economic analysis deriving from the works of Karl Marx and Lenin (see K. Nkrumah, *Neo-colonialism: the Last Stage of Imperialism*, International Publishing Company, 1965; P. Baran and P. Sweezy, *Monopoly Capital*, Penguin, 1973; M. Barratt-Brown, *The Economics of Imperialism*, Penguin, 1973).

There is, however, a significant divergence of viewpoint between those theorists who may be subsumed under the heading of 'dependency theorists'. The majority of such theoreticians would agree with the general view that Third World dependency is the outcome of the global capitalist system; the divergence of view occurs over the precise nature of the exploitation. Some see the lack of development in the Third World as resulting from unequal terms of trade during times of colonial and neo-colonial rule (see A. G. Frank, *Capitalism and Underdevelopment in Latin America*, Monthly Review Press, 1969; A. G. Frank, *Crisis: in the Third World*, Heinemann, 1981; S. Amin, *Accumulation on a World Scale*, Monthly Review Press, 1974).

Other theorists point out the danger of concentrating upon capitalist relations only in terms of market forces. In turn, they indicate that the capitalist *mode* of production, including, as it does, both the *social relations* of production and the nature of the *means* of production together, is an essential part of any analysis of social change (E. Laclau, *Politics and Ideology in Marxist Theory* New Left Books, 1977; G. Taylor, *From Modernization to Modes of Production*, Macmillan Press, 1979). Others have attempted to show how, in the global dimension, through 'aid' packages and the involvement of multinational companies, the economies of the Third World are kept impoverished by the movement of economic resources towards the capitalist centres in the advanced industrial societies (T. Hayter, *Aid as Imperialism*, Penguin, 1971; V. Bornschier, and C. Chase-Dunn, *Transnational Corporations and Underdevelopment*, Praeger, 1985; W. Rodney, *How Europe Underdeveloped Africa*, Bogle-L'Ouverture Publications, 1972). Part 2 of this book sets out to examine critically the views of the dependency theorists and to set the scene for Part 3 in which, by an analysis of actual case studies, it is hoped to show the limitations of each body of theory when confronted with reality. Part 3 critically examines the limits of developmentalist and dependency theories, and concludes by showing how current thinking is attempting to effect a synthesis of the two perspectives through analysis of the role of the state in the more 'successful' Third World nations such as Taiwan.

Finally, in Part 4, an overview is presented of aspects of development having significance for the study of development. In order to help the student formulate views and set the various strands of thought into some coherent whole a number of readings are included, together with some statistical material, to provide a stimulus for further study.

2 Development as evolution: the organic view of society

Sociology emerged as an academic discipline in nineteenth-century Europe against a background of profound and frequently bloody social upheavals. In Britain, what had hitherto been an agrarian society was being transformed into the 'first industrial nation' (Peter Mathias, *The First Industrial Nation*, Methuen, 1969). Throughout the whole of Europe, but especially in France, momentous social events were taking place. The French monarchy was in financial crisis, a situation which indicated even greater economic problems within the country as a whole. Attempts by the government to remedy the situation through increased taxation led to fierce demands for an end to injustice and inequality. These demands were not met and the population became increasingly restless until, soon, a revolution occurred.

The revolution focused the minds of many French intellectuals, not only upon thoughts of Madame Guillotine, but also upon possible causes of the social turmoil which had engulfed their land. One of the first to approach this question from a sociological perspective was an aristocrat, Comte Claude Henri de Saint-Simon (1760–1825). He considered that such serious social problems could only be resolved by a restructuring of the entire economic system. Saint-Simon collaborated closely with his personal secretary, Auguste Comte (1798–1857), on works of social analysis, and in 1822 they jointly published a work entitled *Plan of the Scientific Operations Necessary for the Reorganisation of Society*. This work was typical of the prevailing intellectual climate of the day, *rationalism*, in that analysts used logical reasoning in the interpretation of social events after the collection of information by a process of precise measurement. Natural scientists had developed principles of analysis in which experimental accuracy and observation led to the formulation of laws governing the behaviour of matter in the physical world. Analysts of the social world attempted to follow the same methodological principles in their studies.

In the same way as natural scientists did not concern themselves with the 'meaning' of the behaviour of matter, so the early social 'scientists' conducted the analysis of social events without referring to any meaning which those events might have for people concerned. Social events were thought to be adequate for analysis if they could merely be observed and quantified. This highly objective method of analysing society is called *positivism*. It became, and has remained, a fundamental part of sociological analysis (see Figure 2.1).

Figure 2.1 **Positivism**
The early sociologists held that the social world could be studied in precisely the same way as the world of nature. It was held that social events could be seen as facts capable of being expressed objectively in the form of statistical data, such as birth-rates, death-rates, income levels and so on. By analysing society in this objective way the early social scientists thought that laws governing the behaviour of society could be formulated in the same way as the natural scientists had formulated laws to predict the behaviour of matter.

Following Comte, this approach was developed by another Frenchman, Emile Durkheim, whose social analysis had a profound effect upon the development of sociological analysis in the early twentieth century. Durkheim's work marks a point of transition from the early positivists, who undoubtedly believed that society could be studied in the same way as nature, to more modern interpretations.

More recently in this century, positivism, albeit in a modified form, has flourished principally in the USA with the work of Talcott Parsons. Here sociology is concerned with the analysis of societies as complex units made up of many interconnected components. The elements of social analysis from this perspective are the *structure* and the *function* of the various institutions which make up the whole society and not the individual people within the institutions. In this way objectivity is thought to be assured and positivist scientific tradition maintained by what is called '*structural-functionalist*' analysis.

Positivism has formed the basis of many influential theories within sociology, but accurate measurement of social events alone was found insufficient to provide a satisfactory means of formulating possible laws governing human social behaviour. To attempt this task a further conceptualisation was necessary, and this was provided by viewing society as a living organism.

The organic view of society

It was another widely talented Frenchman, Blaise Pascal (1623–62), with interests which included mathematics (he patented a calculating machine), religion (his *Lettres provinciales* greatly influenced Voltaire), and social analysis, who provided the way forward. He suggested that human society could be likened to an immortal creature which, over the centuries of its existence, constantly added to and refined its store of useful knowledge.

This view of human society as a living organism was not however, entirely new. For example, Shakespeare clearly had the metaphor in mind when in his drama of political turmoil, *Coriolanus*, he gave the following speech to Menenius Agrippa who chastises the citizens of Rome in the following words: 'There was a time when all the body's members/Rebell'd against the belly; thus accus'd it: . . . The senators of Rome are this good belly,/And you the mutinous members' (Act I, Scene 1, lines 94–5; 146–7). The influence of this organic analogy in positivist social analysis has been so influential that, until quite recently, many sociologists have followed what is essentially the same conceptual vision of the social world. In addition, because the organic view of society lent itself so readily to the positivist scientific approach, it acquired a central place in the early sociological analysis of development. In short, then, an entire 'school' of theoretical sociology grew around the positivist-organic view of society and formed the basis of much early developmental sociology. Though such a perspective has been widely challenged and found wanting in many respects, it has left an ideological legacy which may still be seen to underpin many of the attitudes and policies of the governments of the developed world in their relations with the Third World.

Because of its importance, such a theoretical perspective warrants greater attention in order to show more clearly, why, historically, it should have attained such eminence.

Positivist-organic evolutionism

We have seen how, in order to establish laws governing the behaviour of matter, the scientific principles of precise measurement were applied by the positivists to the analysis of society. Also we have seen how the comparison of society with a living

Figure 2.2 **Organic-evolutionary theory**
The theories which use the analogy of the living organism to explain social change make the conceptual link between social and natural science in four ways.

1. Biological organisms change both in size and internal complexity. In other words, as organisms grow and mature, so their internal characteristics are required to become increasingly differentiated and complex. Compare, for example, a single-celled protozoan such as the amoeba with a mammal such as a rabbit. These biological differences can be seen as similar to the observable changes in the social and economic organisation of societies at different stages of 'growth' towards maturity. Thus, primitive societies are less structurally complex than advanced industrial societies.

2 Biological organisms are covered by a restricting layer such as cell wall, skin and so on, which ensures that the organism is maintained as a cohesive, unified and integrated unit. This boundary layer may be represented socially by the assumed consensus of opinion, or agreed moral values, which ensure that individuals in society broadly share the same fundamental beliefs, thereby making certain that harmony prevails.

3 Positivist social analysis has as its objective the formulation of laws relating to development in order accurately to predict future social events.

4 Scientific and positivist social analysis avoid any areas which cannot be incorporated into establishing laws of behaviour. Thus, anything which cannot be measured must be ignored since it does not follow scientific principles of objectivity.

organism – with features such as birth, growth, ageing and death – was used as a way of conceptualising the development of human societies. The influence of this analogy may have been strengthened by the contemporary work of Charles Darwin, whose pronouncements on the process of *biological* evolution brought him into conflict with established tradition.

In Darwin's view the great diversity of life on earth was due to a process he described as 'natural selection', a process whereby specialised development enabled species to adapt to prevailing climatic conditions. Put briefly, his theory stated that those best suited to the environment survived and flourished, while those least fitted perished. This meant that those characteristics of the organism which best fitted it for survival were strengthened, and what resulted was a highly specialised and distinct species carefully adapted to the requirements of a specific environment.

The influence of Darwin's theory of evolution may be seen in the next step in the analysis of social change taken by the early positivist-organic sociologists. Human society was already viewed as akin to a living organism, and, in consequence, societies were similarly thought to pass through evolutionary stages. Thus, in a historical view of societies, those most fitted to prevailing circumstances survived and flourished until, with changes in other variables, they later fell into decline and ultimately perished to be replaced by other societies more suited to the new circumstances.

Evolutionary-organic theorists have produced many works which claim to represent a scientific explanation of the ways various societies have developed. These works, because they were rooted in established scientific tradition, found favour with academic and political elites. In turn, doubtless because of their social and political usefulness in legitimating the existing state of affairs, evolutionary-organic theories have formed the basis of *ideology* (an ideology being a system of beliefs which supports particular behaviour patterns, shapes attitudes, and prescribes the general way a society reacts to outside events). In more recent times this ideological stance has become the operational model for politicians, aid advisers, financiers and investors, as well as for a considerable body of social theoreticians dealing with Third World issues.

3 Organic evolutionary theories of development: functionalism

Auguste Comte (1798–1857)

Comte was the first to use the term 'sociology' (although he preferred his first name for the subject, 'social physics'); he coined the term while attempting to establish the scientific study of human society as an academic discipline in its own right. One of Comte's objectives for this newly formed science was a means of discovering 'through what fixed series of successive transformations the human race, starting from a stage not superior to that of the great apes, gradually led to the point at which civilised Europe finds itself today' (reprinted in *Positive Politics*, vol. IV, trans. Martineau, London, 1875–90, appendix, pp. 149–50).

In 1822 Comte put forward what he termed the 'Law of Three Stages' which, in his view, controlled the evolutionary progression of all societies. Comte declared that all societies effect social progress as a result of the intellectual effort of their citizens – in other words, by the force of ideas. The motivating force for these ideas was, in Comte's view, a rational fear of death which spurred people gradually to improve their control over the forces of nature. Such improvements in the ability to control nature led to a greater survival rate, and therefore the population size increased, which in turn gave rise to yet more problems of survival for the whole society. As more new ideas occurred to meet these new challenges and restore the social equilibrium, so the society gradually progressed along the evolutionary pathway (see Figure 3.1).

Comte's analysis led him to try and promote social progression along the lines suggested by his 'laws'. In his work *A System of Positive Polity* he proposed what he termed a 'religion of humanity', with a clerical hierarchy made up of priest-sociologists – incidentally, he saw himself in the role of High-Priest – whose task it was to ensure that social life was maintained in accordance with a new moral code.

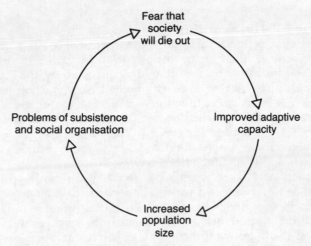

Figure 3.1   Comte's cycle of social development

Of central importance to Comte's work is the principle of social evolution through the force of ideas which adapt human beings in society to new circumstances and themselves initiate further change. In this respect Comte may be seen as the forerunner of many other theorists who built upon his path-breaking work – among them, Emile Durkheim.

Emile Durkheim (1858–1917)

Durkheim, who is often called the 'father of functionalism' (see Figure 3.2), owes much to the earlier work of Comte; indeed, it is possible to identify a common theme in their respective analyses which threads through the whole of functionalist theory. As Anthony Giddens has remarked:

> The overlapping interpretations which Saint-Simon and Comte offered of the decline of feudalism and the emergence of the modern form of society constitute the principal foundation for the whole of Durkheim's writings.
>
> (A. Giddens, *Capitalism and Modern Social Theory*, CUP, 1974, p. 65)

Figure 3.2 **Functionalism**

Functionalist social analysis developed from, and relies heavily upon, the organic analogy used by earlier theorists. In the same way as the natural sciences study the living organism by referring to its component parts, such as heart, lungs and brain, what function each performs and how they interact together for the good of the whole, so functionalist sociologists examine society in terms of component institutions – for example, family, trade unions, churches and so on – and their function in society.

Functionalists see society as a *social system* made up of a series of interconnected parts. These parts, or *institutions*, are made up of individuals, but it is the institutions which are of prime importance in social analysis since individuals within them are controlled in their behaviour by an agreed pattern of *rules* and *laws*. Thus, while individual human beings may change, the structure within which they function remains to be measured and evaluated objectively. A social system is, therefore, a complex of institutions, each providing a function for the benefit of the society as a whole. For the system to continue in being, it is necessary for all the different parts to co-exist in a state of harmony, a condition which is maintained by what is termed a '*value consensus*'.

The idea of 'shared values' lies at the heart of functionalist theory, since it forms a foundation for social unity and cohesion which is central to functionalist analysis. Functionalists explain the acquisition of this 'value consensus' by stressing the process of socialisation whereby the norms and values of a society are learned (internalised) by individuals, thus ensuring social conformity and, hence, control.

Functionalists argue that effective social control can only be maintained if individuals submit to the greater authority of 'society' itself. Individuals fulfil their allotted role within a social institution which is thought to operate in promoting the general good of the whole social system. A common culture (value consensus) binds the whole system together – a situation strengthened by the interdependence of institutions, owing to each having become so specialised that they could not survive independently.

It is clear that Comte and Durkheim share the functionalist belief in a social equilibrium brought about by an agreed value consensus which is thought to underpin the whole social system. In addition, Durkheim also followed Comte and the evolutionists in viewing society *holistically*; that is, by emphasising the importance of social institutions and discounting individuals as irrelevant to social analysis. For Durkheim, individuals in society appear as passive, empty vessels to be filled with the normative social values which make up the particular value consensus in the society. Only after internalising these group values would each individual in a society behave in accordance with identifiable (and predictable) group behaviour patterns. The social system which resulted from this process would, Durkheim envisaged, be existing in a condition of both harmony and equilibrium.

Durkheim's first published work was his doctoral thesis, entitled 'The Division of Labour in Society' (1893), which has as its theme the fundamental division between what he called '*traditional*' (primitive) societies and '*modern*' (industrial) societies. Durkheim analysed the complex variety of these societies by compressing them into broad generalities, but, nevertheless, his work is of great interest and importance, for it attempts an understanding of the *process* of development as well as cataloguing the stages of development.

A fundamental question for Durkheim was, therefore, by what means are societies maintained largely in a state of order? Further, upon what basis does this order rest while the society undergoes evolutionary change into an increasingly complex organisational form? To answer these questions Durkheim examined many different societies, and noted that, in all cases, as each society evolved it became more internally differentiated. After industrialisation, production was no longer carried out within the family unit since most people went out to work in factories or other large-scale organisations. This situation promoted the growth of other social institutions in order to replace the loss of traditional extended family support. These institutions developed into professional specialisms which provided further areas of work for people in society. In his analysis Durkheim used the variety of internal differentiation between societies as a means of comparing their evolutionary progress.

In traditional (simple) societies there was only limited internal differentiation, and individuals were bound together socially by what Durkheim called *'mechanical solidarity'*. He described this as a pattern of behaviour resulting from individuals in society following a pattern of rules established by tradition, custom or habit. Individuals are seen as sharing a consensus of social norms and values which Durkheim termed the 'conscience collective'. Societies exhibiting mechanical solidarity were identified as small kinship groups in which all subscribe to the same overall pattern of values and beliefs. These groups, Durkheim thought, were capable of self-sufficiency because they were relatively undifferentiated in their means of production – as, for example, in agrarian tribal cultures.

Durkheim noted that societies followed an evolutionary path away from these traditional forms of organisation towards industrialisation, which, he claimed, exhibited *'organic solidarity'*. This form of social cohesion he saw as arising from the necessity of interdependence between institutions brought about by increased specialisation of function and division of labour in the system of production. The 'conscience collective' which typified the simpler social systems vanished as internal differentiation increased; instead of agreed co-operation between individuals, there developed a different form of social interaction based upon specialised differentials of function between individuals. In modern complex society people co-operate because they are forced to do so by the nature of the system of production and the external constraints upon them from the law. In consequence, the main emphasis of human social activity in modern society is diverted away from group solidarity and towards selfish interest.

Durkheim employed the organic analogy with increasing emphasis as he extended his evolutionary analysis. He noted that, with an increase in population, social institutions become more numerous and functionally specific. Thus, in Durkheim's analysis, development appears to become synonymous with an increase in the internal complexity of social organisation. Here he encountered a significant theoretical problem for, with the growth in the division of labour and the reduction in the 'traditional' bonds which bind individuals together socially, the equilibrium of the social system appears at risk. There is an apparent conflict between what Durkheim called the 'cult of the individual' and the social solidarity which the acceptance of a value consensus previously ensured. Durkheim noted that complex modern society developed specialised legal systems which allowed both civil and criminal actions to be brought against offenders.

Durkheim may, therefore, be seen as having begun the movement away from a concern simply to establish general lists of the stages of social evolution (the *how* of development) towards a concern with the internal changes underlying the stages (the *why* of development). This is no minor shift of emphasis, since it moves the focus of analysis towards attempting to come to terms with the whole question of social change, and explaining the different rates of development between societies. This change in emphasis has required functionalist theoreticians to search for a new evolutionary perspective, and it is to this that we now turn.

Talcott Parsons (1902–79)

The effect of interaction between a society which has experienced change and other societies in an unchanged, traditional form of social organisation can be seen analysed theoretically in the work of the eminent American sociologist Talcott Parsons (often referred to as the founder of modern functionalism). For over fifty years, since the publication in 1937 of his first major work, *The Structure of Social Action*, Parsons has been (arguably) the most prolific and controversial figure in American sociology. He is seen by many as the 'arch-functionalist' in that his work is based upon the premise that social life generally is conducted through 'mutual advantage and peaceful co-operation rather than mutual hostility and destruction'.

Central importance in Parsons' sociology is given to the 'functioning of structures', and, accordingly, he views all societies as systems made up of differentiated, functionally specific social institutions. The whole system is maintained in a state of harmonious equilibrium by an agreed value consensus.

So for Parsons, like Durkheim, the main concern of sociological analysis is the scientific study of social institutions (interestingly, Durkheim once defined sociology as 'the science of institutions'). In Parsons' view, social institutions are seen as distinct, though interdependent, groups having broadly similar cultural patterns. Following Durkheim, Parsons explained the similarity of cultural patterns as resulting from two sources of influence:

1 through a process of socialisation, in which the individual internalises group norms and value systems;

2 through external social controls, whereby individuals are under threat of punishment if they deviate from prescribed legal patterns of behaviour.

Parsons viewed all social systems as facing quite specific problems in order to survive and flourish. He set out four conditions which he claimed were fundamentals in the survival of any social system. These he has termed the 'Functional prerequisites' or 'imperatives' of survival.

1 Adaptation

This is the process by which social systems interact with their surrounding natural environment to provide the basic needs of food, clothing and shelter.

2 Integration

The social system has established patterns of social behaviour which ensure that it is harmonious and stable.

3 Goal attainment

The social system has aims representing socially valuable functions which are to be adequately rewarded.

4 Latency

This is concerned with the social system ensuring that the institutional values are kept and social order is maintained.

All four items mentioned by Parsons are closely interconnected and, consequently, any change in one aspect will produce a compensatory change in some or all of the others. As Parsons himself observes: 'Once a disturbance has been introduced into an equilibrated system there will tend to be a reaction to this disturbance which tends to restore the system to equilibrium' (T. Parsons, The Social System, Free Press, 1951). It is in the process of restoring equilibrium to the social system that the process of social change occurs. Parsons, finding a typically functionalist difficulty in using the word 'change', chose to call this process 'moving equilibrium'.

In the 1960s Parsons turned his attention towards the process of social evolution. In an article for the American Sociological Review (23(3) June 1964, 339), he stated that the 'emphasis in both sociological and anthropological quarters is shifting from a studied disinterest in problems of social and cultural evolution . . . to an evolutionary framework'. As a foundation for his analysis Parsons proposed the concept of 'evolutionary universals'. This he defined as 'any organizational development sufficiently important to further evolution, that, rather than emerging only once, it is likely to be "hit upon" by various systems operating under different conditions' (ibid.).

Evolutionary universals are, according to Parsons, fundamental requirements in order for social systems to effect a movement in their equilibrium. According to his theoretical scheme they will 'endow their possessors with a very substantial increase in generalized adaptive capacity, so substantial that species lacking in them are relatively disadvantaged in the major areas in which natural selection operates, not so much for survival as for the opportunity to initiate further major developments' (ibid., 356).

Among the evolutionary universals noted by Parsons is the growth within the social system of a legitimated differentiation of function away from the confines of the family. Additionally, this functional differentiation must form into a clearly apparent system of social stratification. Another vital universal is the formation of a written language system, since this will tend to ensure that one group will separate from another hierarchically through access to literacy. This separation will provide a power base upon which to legitimise the stratification system – a situation which may be enhanced through an effective bureaucratic system. Other universals mentioned by Parsons include a monetary economy and a market system underpinned by a comprehensive legal framework which has widespread acceptance in the social system.

In Parsons' view, the evolution of societies must be seen as a rather haphazard process resulting from 'cultural diffusion' between those systems on a higher evolutionary plane and those at a lower level. Parsons has defined specific societies which, in his opinion, represent the stages through which societies must pass on their evolutionary path.

Primitive	Aboriginal (undifferentiated)
Ancient primitive and archaic	Ancient Egypt
Historic intermediate	Ancient India, China
'Seed-bed'	Ancient Israel, Greece and Rome
Modern	Industrial USA and Europe

Each of these successive stages, Parsons maintained, is charac-
terised by the introduction of certain 'evolutionary universals',
such as language, monetary economy and so on. Parsons has
stressed two of these universals which, in his view, are crucial to
the process of social evolution from the primitive stage. The first
of these is the decline of traditional kinship patterns such as the
extended family. The second is a situation where, in Parsons' own
words, the development of a well-marked system of social stratification 'comes first and is a condition of legitimation of political
function' (*The Social System*, p. 342). In other words, social systems
must be structured so that people are unequal both in terms of
wealth and access to power. Such a situation, Parsons envisaged,
would ensure effective leadership of the masses by those most fitted
to perform that function.

Here Parsons encountered the same difficulty as Durkheim.
With the growth of internal complexity and the movement towards
individualism, which is seen as typifying industrial society, how
can both the equilibrium and the dynamism of the social system
be maintained at the same time? Dynamism will be introduced by
individualism, but this will erode the supposed value consensus
and threaten the equilibrium; a return to value consensus will
inhibit individualism and restrict dynamism. The two aspects of
society seem to be incompatible.

Parsons resolved the dilemma by claiming that the increased
diversity of institutions allows social values to become more *generalised* throughout the whole system. For example, Parsons claimed
that there are universal standards of basic morality, together with
widespread acceptance of such values as competition, achievement,
freedom under the law and so on throughout Western industrial
society. These 'generalised social values' and the movement to
'enhance adaptive capacity' also require, in Parsons' view, an
effective education system and mass-media communication
network in order that ideas can be diffused throughout other social
systems.

In Parsons' analysis these ideas diffuse outwards from the
centres of industrialisation (these he identified as the Western
nations) in a gradual, evolutionary way. In this Parsons followed
Max Weber in the observation that the industrial system in itself
brings about similar patterns of social organisation in social
systems. Many theorists have followed a similar line in declaring
that as a society progresses towards the industrial mode of

production and assumes the internal characteristics of complex, modern society, it may be said to experience development. Theorists differ in the emphasis which they give to the role either of ideas or of technology in bringing about the adoption of an industrial mode of production.

Many are in agreement, however, on the requirement that simple societies must modernise (that is, they must effect industrialisation) in order to be said to have undergone development, and so this group of analysts are known collectively as *modernisation theorists*. Having traced the theoretical heritage of the modernisation theorists, in the next chapter we will examine the main features of this body of theory and will try to assess its impact upon the debate surrounding development.

4 Developmentalist theory: modernisation

From their analyses of social systems, some theorists have maintained that the historical progression of societies has always been from simple, undifferentiated systems to complex, highly differentiated systems; the most complex of these being modern industrial society. In addition, many of these same theorists tend to accept the convergence thesis view that all industrial societies, irrespective of political affiliation, tend to adopt similar forms of social organisation. Thus developmental progress comes to be seen as a process of acquiring the characteristics of modern industrial society. Indeed, one of the fundamental parts of developmentalist theory is the belief that traditional cultural, social and political structures in the Third World preclude the growth of effective economic strategies. Only if these barriers to advancement are removed, it is claimed, will the societies be able to become developed.

In economic terms the developmentalist approach is based upon the assumption that a free market economy compounded by an entrepreneurial enterprise culture (currently much in vogue through 'Thatcherism' and 'Reaganomics' throughout the Western economies) will, as in Britain during the period of the Industrial Revolution, bring about a major 'take-off into growth'.

Modernisation theorists who follow this perspective claim that societies are relatively poor and underdeveloped because they lack the internal structural characteristics suitable for the introduction of the industrial system. Among such characteristics lacking in these poorer societies are, it is claimed, investment capital and entrepreneurial values, together with the modern technological equipment and the necessary skills to use them effectively. It is further suggested that the less developed societies can be helped towards 'enhanced adaptive capacity' (a functionalist euphemism for social change) by a process of interaction with the more advanced nations.

Many modernisation theorists have suggested ways in which simple, agrarian societies in the Third World may be helped in establishing the industrial system of production. Eminent among these analysts is W. W. Rostow, an American economist whose work *The Stages of Economic Growth* (CUP, 1969), examines the patterns of social change which, historically, have led to modern industrial societies. Having isolated technology as the key to progress, he attempts to provide 'an account of economic growth, based on a dynamic theory of production and interpreted in terms of actual societies'.

The fact that his work is subtitled *A Non-Communist Manifesto* would tend to indicate that Rostow is scarcely concerned to produce an objective analysis. However, in spite of this (or maybe because of this!), it has been received with widespread acclaim and general acceptance throughout the academic and political institutions of Western industrial nations. Such a situation may be due to the fact that Rostow provides a theoretical justification for the policies which govern relations between the developed and less developed nations. Rostow's work appears effectively to combine both the neo-classical free-market economist theoreticians' views and the work of the modernisation theorists.

A summary of Rostow's model of how nations may progress can be given thus:

Stage 1 The traditional society   A poor society with subsistence agriculture; a simple, undifferentiated system of social organisation in which mysticism and religions play a large part.

Stage 2 The preconditions for take-off   Population increases, due to the advances made in agriculture, and this allows more workers to be involved in developing transport and power supplies.

Stage 3 Take-off into economic growth   Manufacturing industry grows and encourages more workers to enter the secondary sector of the economy.

Stage 4 The drive to maturity   The wealth produced from the developed industrial system facilitates even more industrial growth. In addition the infrastructure, such as health care and education, is improved.

Stage 5 The stage of mass high consumption   Industry makes a change of emphasis from the production of basic commodities such as steel, machinery, textiles and so on, to supplying consumer goods such as washing machines, television sets and high-technology luxuries.

Rostow has indicated that, in his view, there are two main factors involved in the process of changing simple, traditional societies into modern, industrial-production systems. First, there are non-economic factors (such as attitudes and ideas) which involve an acceptance of entrepreneurial values whereby

> a new elite – a new leadership – must emerge and be given scope to begin the building of a modern industrial society; and, while the Protestant Ethic by no means represents a set of values uniquely suitable for modernization, it is essential that the members of this new elite regard modernization as a possible task, serving some end they judge to be ethically good or otherwise advantageous.
>
> Sociologically this new elite must – to a degree – supersede in social and political authority the old land-based elite.
>
> (Rostow, *The Stages of Economic Growth*, p. 26)

Here Rostow advocated that the dominant values of the advanced societies (entrepreneurialism, competition, individualism and so on) must be introduced into the less developed societies. One way in which this could be done is by installing into the large centres of population in such societies a local elite made up of nationals who have internalised the value system of the advanced society. Once such a group acquire and maintain control over the society, the installation of the required institutions and organisational system is comparatively simple.

Rostow also indicated certain economic factors which, he maintained, are necessary for the change from simple to complex industrial society. These factors he has separated into two categories:

> 1 men . . . must be prepared to lend their money on long term, at high risk, to back the innovating entrepreneurs – not in money lending, playing the exchanges, foreign trade or real estate – but in modern industry . . . .
>
> 2 agriculture must supply more food. Food is needed to meet the likely rise in population, without yielding either starvation or a depletion of foreign exchange available for purposes essential to growth . . . . In short, an environment of rising real incomes in agriculture, rooted in increased productivity, may be an important stimulus to new modern industrial

> sectors essential to the take-off . . . agriculture must yield up a substantial part of its surplus income to the modern sector.
> Rostow, *The Stages of Economic Growth*, pp. 20–4)

The relative poverty of the less developed societies, according to Rostow and other developmentalist theoreticians,* arises from a lack of capital available for investment to finance new (industrial) methods of production. The population of the poorer society is unable to raise any of this capital themselves, and so, Rostow asserted, the developed societies should inject capital in order to provide the stimulus and the basis for economic growth. The wealth created by such growth will reduce overall poverty and enable further development to occur, further enhancing the economic progress of the society. It is possible, in Rostow's view, for some of the capital to be created from the agricultural sector of the developing society, but, he fears, this will not itself be at a sufficient level of efficiency until it has become organised on industrial lines.

Rostow has tended to stress the importance of capital equipment and technology in the process of effecting change from simple social structures to complex industrial forms. He does not make clear, however, how the capital and technological skills are to be introduced into the developing societies. It is also not clear whether the capital injection is to be made in the form of a donation or a loan.

Modernisation theorists, in their zeal to enhance the economic growth of the Third World, have emphasised the need for industrialisation. In so doing they have provided an invaluable foundation upon which the politicians and financiers of the developed world build the shelter to hide their real ideological intent. As Hoogvelt has remarked:

> structural-functionalist theories of modernisation have in fact very usefully served as an ideological mask camouflaging the imperialist nature of Western capitalism. The Western capitalist

---

* See also E. E. Hagen, *The Economics of Development*, 3rd edn, Homewood, IL: R. Irwin 1980; M. Olson, *The Rise and Decline of Nations*, New Haven, CT: Yale University Press, 1982; G. Gilder, *The Spirit of Enterprise*, New York: Simon & Schuster, 1984; and A. Inkeles, *Exploring Individual Modernity*, New York: Columbia University Press, 1983.

system for its very own survival needed and still needs to expand.

(A. M. M. Hoogvelt, *The Sociology of Developing Societies*, Macmillan, 1983, pp. 61–2)

Attempts to clear away some of this camouflage and to expose the true character of the relationship between the developed and developing world have been made by analysts viewing from another, contrary, perspective. Approaching the question of underdevelopment from a diametrically opposite position to the developmentalists, they see Third World poverty as the logical outcome of the exploitative character of international capitalism. The main theoretical ground upon which these analysts have based their investigations is derived largely from the work of Karl Marx. In consequence, in order to provide a basis for our own examination of their contribution to the study of social development, we must first outline the relevant features of Marx's work.

PART 2

Dependency theory

5   Development as dependency

One perspective on the analysis of development – that of developmentalist/modernisation theory – seeks, as we have seen, to measure the structural changes which occur within individual societies, and to use this as a means of determining the degree of development which has taken place. In other words, those societies having, for example, a higher gross national product or increased level of technology and organisational complexity than others are to be viewed as more developed. In the view of opposing theorists this perspective fails to take full account of the historical evidence of contact between societies.

A superficial examination of the historical evidence indicates, in their view, that societies have not developed in isolation. The whole of human history is filled with examples of nations conquering and subduing others to their will in order to exploit both their resources and their people. The idea that the attitudes and the technology necessary for industrialisation would spread by a process of benevolent diffusion has been seriously challenged by many theorists of a Marxist complexion. Marx's work is of importance because it provides a way of analysing social change in terms of economic relationships *between* social systems. To understand the work of theorists writing from this perspective it is first necessary briefly to outline the main features of Marx's analysis.

Karl Marx (1818–1883)

Karl Marx achieved fame (some would say notoriety) for his

analysis of the pattern of economic relationships which he identified as the foundation of all other human social relations. Marx's analysis is, however, considerably more than sociological, because he provides a practical agenda for changing society through revolutionary action. His is not merely a passive analysis; it is an active process promoting social change which, during his lifetime and to the present day, has initiated much working-class action. In consequence, he was banished from country after country (Germany on 16 May 1849 and from France on 14 June 1849) eventually finding sanctuary in London, where he wrote many of his greatest works, including *Capital*, which was never finished due to his death.

Marx began from the premise that individuals in society are required to satisfy the basic human needs for food, clothing and shelter in order to survive. It is in the process of satisfying these material necessities that, according to Marx, human beings enter into social and economic relationships with one another, and it is the nature of these relationships which changes as the process of satisfying the needs alters. This is the foundation of Marx's analysis; that human social life is founded upon the nature of the system of economic relations at any given time.

Marx's theoretical scheme has given social scientists a powerful, radical alternative to the functionalist perspective. This was made clear by Engels, a lifelong friend of Marx, when, in a speech at Marx's graveside on 17 March 1883, he declared that 'Just as Darwin discovered the law of development of organic nature so Marx discovered the law of development of human history' (K. Marx and F. Engels, *Selected Works*, Lawrence & Wishart, 1970, p. 429).

For Marx the material basis of society determines and conditions an individual's social being. In this Marx is emphasising the role of material conditions in the process of social change, a view which contradicts Weber's emphasis on ideas as the most significant factor in the process. As Engels himself declared:

> in every society that has appeared in history . . . the final causes of all social changes and political revolutions are to be sought, not in men's brains, not in men's better insight into eternal truth and justice, but in the changes in the modes of production and exchange.
> (Marx and Engels, *Selected Works*, p. 411).

Each form of social organisation (other than early communistic societies) may thus be seen, for Marx, as typified by various patterns of conflict between opposing social groups. He has outlined 'Asiatic, Ancient, Feudal and Modern Bourgeois' as 'progressive epochs in the economic formation of society' (ibid., p. 182). Indeed, Marx and Engels claim in a famous passage that conflict has been, and continues to be, a consistent phenomenon throughout all stage of human society:

> The history of all hitherto existing society is the history of class struggles. . . . Our epoch, the epoch of the bourgeoisie, possesses, however, this distinctive feature: it has simplified the class antagonisms. Society as a whole is more and more splitting up into two great hostile camps into two great classes directly facing each other: Bourgeoisie and Proletariat.
> (Ibid., pp. 35–6)

Thus, for Marx, every capitalist society has within it a system of exploitative relations founded upon the pattern of social relationships of production (that is, class relations) determined by the nature of the productive process. These social relations of productions form one component of the productive process. Together with the *means* of production (which, of course, vary widely throughout history and between nations) they form what Marx termed the *mode of production*. Marx claimed that societies can be analysed in terms of the nature of the mode of production within them. Once this is known, then, according to Marx, it is possible to determine the nature of the society since each change in the mode of production necessarily produces corresponding changes in the patterns of social relations.

Marx outlined four main stages which, he declared, follow on from primitive communism. These are, 'Asiatic, Ancient, Feudal and Modern Bourgeois' (Marx, Preface to 'The Critique of Political Economy' in Marx and Engels, *Selected Works*). The 'Modern Bourgeois' stage is reached, according to Marx, when the

> feudal system of industry, under which industrial production was monopolised by closed guilds, now no longer sufficed for the growing wants of the new markets. The manufacturing system took its place. The guild-masters were pushed on one side by the manufacturing middle class. . . Meantime the

markets kept ever growing, the demand ever rising. Even manufacture no longer sufficed. . . . The place of manufacture was taken by the giant, Modern Industry.

(Marx and Engels, 'Manifesto of the Communist Party', in *Selected Works*, pp. 36–7)

Marx acknowledged that the industrial system was, potentially, the great saviour and liberator of human kind. He saw it as a system capable of providing an improved quality of life for all, but, in Marx's interpretation, there was one significant problem which would prevent the industrial system from achieving its full potential. This problem, he maintained, was the capitalist system. This mode of production – industrial capitalism – is a system in which the wealth produced becomes the sole property of a minority, capital-owning group. At the same time, the producers of wealth – a majority which Marx described as 'wage slaves' – are held in a condition of subjection and relative poverty. This, according to Marx, forms the essence of capitalist social relationships.

Under industrial capitalism Marx identified the emergence of two great classes: a minority class of manufacturing capitalists which he called the 'bourgeoisie'; and a far larger class of industrial workers which he called the 'proletariat'. The rapid growth of towns, together with a massed urbanised workforce in the giant factories, provided, in Marx's view, an arena for the growth of class conflict.

The capitalist bourgeoisie who owned the means of production, and the landless proletariat who owned nothing save their labour power, were the two opposing halves of the equation of industrial production. In this process of production, according to Marx, the proletariat change raw materials into usable commodities, thereby increasing the value of the raw material. In return, the proletariat receive wages from the bourgeoisie, who thus lay claim to the finished product – which they sell in the market-place at a profit.

Marx calculated that the wages paid by the bourgeoisie were always fixed at a level lower than the cost of production. Thus the bourgeoisie made profit twice: once from what Marx called 'surplus value' – that is, the difference between labour costs and the value of the commodity; second, they profited at the retail sale of the finished product to the consumer.

Marx goes on, in his analysis of the capitalist system of

production, to show how economic relationships compel capitalists constantly to seek greater and greater profits. In order to do this they are forced to compete with one another, and, in consequence, small enterprises are swallowed up by larger ones in order to increase profits by reducing competition and by increased economies of scale. Accordingly, as more and more of the proletariat gathered in the same place of work, Marx thought that individual workers would become conscious of their common interests and form a 'class grouping' and, realising their power as a unified class, that they would rise up and overthrow the bourgeoisie by revolutionary action. After a period known as the 'dictatorship of the proletariat' during which, Marx envisaged, people would become re-socialised into co-operative instead of competitive social values, the oppressive state apparatus of capitalism would 'wither away' and be followed by a classless Utopian society – the stage of communism.

More modern analysts have produced revisions of Marx's theoretical scheme and have attempted to apply them to events in the contemporary world. These 'neo-Marxist approaches' (see A. Foster-Carter, 'Neo-Marxist Approaches to Development and Underdevelopment', in E. de Kadt and C. Williams (eds) *Sociology and Development*, Tavistock, 1974) extend and broaden the scope of Marx's analysis of capitalist relationships *within* societies to include the analysis of social relations *between* societies. Put briefly, from this analytical perspective capitalist industrial societies are seen to have obtained, and to have maintained, their affluence through exploitative relationships with the less developed societies. Marx himself indicated something of this process in his statement that

> The need of a constantly expanding market for its products chases the bourgeoisie over the whole surface of the globe. It must nestle everywhere, establish connections everywhere. The bourgeoisie has through its exploitation of the world-market given a cosmopolitan character to production and consumption in every county. . . . In place of the old wants, satisfied by the productions of the country, we find new wants, requiring for their satisfaction the products of distant lands and climes.
> (Marx and Engels, *Selected Works*, p. 39).

It was Lenin who first moved the analytical focus on from Marx's work and began to view the effects of capitalist interaction in the

Figure 5.1 **A dialectic**
A dialectic is a philosophical concept which involves the determination of knowledge by a process of logical questioning. Hegel, an eminent German philosopher, developed this principle and applied it to the relationship of ideas. The process, briefly put, can be explained in the following way. An idea is proposed – this is the *thesis*; a differing, or opposing, idea is then proposed in discussion – this is the *anti-thesis*. From ensuing discussion or debate a compromise idea is reached which includes elements of each – this is the *synthesis*. In a continual process of change this synthesis then forms the *thesis* in later discussions, and so the dialectical progression continues.

Marx adapted the Hegelian form of the dialectic and applied it to the material world. For Marx it was matter or, more specifically, mankind's relationship with matter, which provides the motive power for development. It was from his analysis of capitalism in this way that Marx pronounced upon the relationship between the mode of production holding primacy in any given era and the nature of the social formations produced within it. Thus, according to Marx, the development of a specific culture within human society is dependent upon the nature of the dialectical relationship between the economic and social contradictions of capitalism. The bourgeoisie are in an antithetical relationship with the proletariat, which, following struggles, ultimately results in the formation of a new form of social organisation.

world as a whole. Lenin observed the tendency for capitalist nations forcibly to take raw materials from, and to sell finished products to, other nations which they held in a position of subjection. This process Lenin called 'imperialism', which he described as 'the highest stage in the development of capitalism, one in which production has assumed such big, immense proportions that free competition gives way to monopoly. That is the economic essence of imperialism. . . . Economically, imperialism is monopoly capitalism' ('A Caricature of Marxism and Imperialist Economism', in Lenin, *On the USA*, Moscow: Progress Publishers, 1967, pp. 290–1). Lenin went further, in the same work, to examine the ways in which capitalist enterprises gain access to, and control of, the economies of other nations. He suggests that this is achieved through a rival's financial dependence and acquisition of his sources of raw materials and eventually of all his enterprises (ibid., p. 291).

The process by which the advanced industrial nations are seen to have subjected and exploited non-industrial societies is seen, by analysts of a neo-Marxist persuasion, as a 'dialectic' (see Figure 5.1) The resulting synthesis produces a condition in which the dominated society is made to be dependent upon the more powerful society in many ways: through systematic exploitation and frequently harsh, even brutal, oppression the links in the chains which bind the oppressed nation are forged. Such a sequence of events can be observed throughout the whole of human history so that wars, invasions and other conquests (through trading and commerce, for example), have gradually formed the nations of the earth into a globally stratified hierarchy of affluence and power.

From a Marxist perspective, therefore, relations between nations – as between individuals – can be seen as the affluent maintaining, and adding to, their prosperity, while the poorer remain subjected, dependent and in relative poverty due to the exploitative pattern of relationships within capitalism. With Marx's and Lenin's theoretical scheme as a background we now turn to more recent social analyses from a similar perspective.

6 Colonialism, imperialism and neo-colonialism

As the industrialised nations developed economically they increased not only in affluence but also in size of population and complexity of internal structural differentiation. These conditions increased the overall standard of life for the people, which, in turn, created expanded markets for the produce of overseas countries that merchant-traders brought back to their shores.

A major difficulty for the continued success of such commercial ventures during this early period was the often unreliable nature of the supply resulting from the haphazard nature of the agrarian mode of production and, significantly, from the system of social organisation in the supplying nations. In order to overcome this, and to ensure a more stabilised pattern of production, the powerful commercial and political elites in the industrialised nations set about changing the economic, social and political systems of the less developed nations. These changes were necessary, as they saw it, to create a socio-economic organisation which would be more congruent with that of the developed; a situation which would enhance the commercial efficiency of the relationship between the two nations.

To transform the structure of the less developed society into a more commercially beneficial form it was necessary for the developed nations' elite to install members of their own society into positions of authority within the subject economy. This process often met with some local resistance and, occasionally, open hostility, which was immediately put down by armed force if necessary. Gradually some members of the subject population became dependent upon the developed society for their livelihood and socialised into its norms and values. This created a dual society within the dominated nation; one group, an elite, having a higher level of income and power and giving allegiance to the foreign nationals; another group, the great mass of people, living in poverty and being controlled by the first group. Such a situation meant that the foreign interventionists could, effectively, be seen to have no overt controlling influence while, at the same time, ensuring that relations between the two nations gradually entered a relatively harmonious, if grossly unequal, phase – that of colonialism.

It is perhaps a mistake to describe this phase as a 'trading relationship' since this implies that the colonised were acting voluntarily. Under colonialism, the people of the colonised society were under the ever-increasing control of the colonising power. This pattern of domination resulted in conditions which were frequently little short of slavery or, at best, enforced exploitation, in which the wages paid to colonial workers were always much lower than those paid to their counterparts in the developed nations.

Trading companies whose commercial dealings relied upon the cash crops produced by native labour were anxious to increase output and maintain low price levels. Thanks to the prudent management of native labour, production in colonial territories increased rapidly in order to meet the growing demand of the market in the advanced nations. In some, comparatively rare, instances, relations between colonial and colonised may have been of a benign, paternalist nature, but it must be said that, generally, colonised peoples were frequently subject to brutal treatment with the aim of increasing production of commodities which the colonising power needed to expand its domestic industrial economy.

Through the process of colonialism, the advanced industrial nations imposed their own social, economic and cultural values, and, in a comparatively short period of time, many people from industrialised nations began to settle in the colonies. This consolidated the process of transformation by which the mode of production of the colonised society would be changed. In addition, as the mode of production changed, so too did the legal, political and cultural superstructure of the colonised society become modified to accept the normative values of the colonial power. Nowhere is this more apparent than in the process by which colonising European nations introduced a cash economy into what had previously been a mainly bartering or exchange economy in the nations they colonised. This had a two-fold effect.

First, it enabled the colonial power to impose a form of taxation upon the colonised peoples in order to raise cash revenue to finance improvement projects. This strengthened the hand of the colonisers, for it meant that 'cash' money had to be earned somehow in order to pay the taxes. Individuals were therefore compelled to grow cash crops for sale (at highly advantageous rates) to the European traders, or they had to offer their labour for sale on the plantations or industrial enterprises owned and controlled by Europeans. The latter situation led to wage levels being held down to only marginally above the level of taxation.

Second, by introducing the currency of the colonial nation into the colony and ensuring that the colonised people used it for all trading with overseas nations (usually the colonial power itself!), the colonisers were able to exert tremendous controls over the colonies by virtue of having power over the rate of exchange (see H. Magdoff, *The Age of Imperialism*, Monthly Review Press, 1969).

Early colonialism thus progressed to a stage in which the dominant power had effectively produced a replica of its own economic and social pattern of organisation within colonised society. The colonised people gradually adopted, by a process of enforced socialisation, the value system and mode of production of the colonial power. It was, however, much more than this in practical terms, for, in the colonies, capitalism could be employed in a much purer, starker form unfettered by the constraints of opposition in the form of organised labour movements, or political ideologies, which compromised the pursuit of profit in the domestic nation. Such a situation ensured massive capital investment from the centre to the colonies; investment which enabled capitalist enterprises to develop into huge monopolies making, in the process, vast profits for a minority of speculators in the industrialised nations.

What were the results of this process and what legacy has been left in terms of development for the colonised society? It can be seen that, as a result of colonisation, the internal structure and the overall size of the economy grew in the colonised societies generally. Thus, analysis of any specific society from a purely quantitative, functionalist perspective could conclude that it had undergone a process of development. In qualitative terms, however, conditions for the people within such a society may be seen rather differently: as either stagnant, or even retrogressive, with a reduction in elements such as personal freedom and living standards. Whatever wealth was left within the society was always further divided unequally, with a minority growing relatively wealthy while the majority remained in poverty or destitution.

1 Can developing societies make independent progress towards industrialisation?

In an interesting article ('Imperialism and Capitalist Industrialization', *New Left Review* 81, Sept.–Oct. 1973), Bill Warren has presented evidence claiming to show that substantial and sustained independent progress towards industrialisation can be made within under-developed nations. He has based his argument upon a comparison of manufacturing output in countries of the Third World with those of the developed areas. What Warren appears to show is that colonialism is not a necessarily exploitative relationship, for, once set on the pathway to industrialisation, previously colonised societies can achieve unfettered development, which, by implication, means an increase in the overall quality of life. He has concluded that

> private investment in the Third World is increasingly creating the conditions for the disappearance of imperialism as a system of economic inequality between nations of the capitalist world system, and that there are no limits, in principle, to this process. Thus imperialism conceived as an unequal system of surplus creation and extraction is self-destructive.
> (Bill Warren, ibid., 40)

The validity of his observations have been challenged by others (see, for example, *New Left Review* 85, May/June 1974, 83–104) on the grounds that it is necessary to view not merely *gross* economic growth, but also the way in which such growth is distributed throughout the population in terms of increased living standards and level of democracy. However, by referring to the earlier discussion on the *positivist tradition* in sociology (which, it may be remembered, lies at the basis of the *functionalist analysis*), observant readers will have little difficulty in understanding Warren's emphasis upon overall *economic growth*.

The equation of 'development' with economic growth is of significance for functionalist analysis, because it permits analysts to be distanced from human suffering by the study of clinical columns of figures which show higher gross national product and enhanced rates of production etc. As Dudley Seers has remarked in a thought-provoking article:

> now that the complexity of development problems is becoming increasingly obvious, this continued addiction to the use of a

single aggregative indicator in the face of the evidence, takes on a rather different appearance. It begins to look like a preference for avoiding the real problems of development.

(Dudley Seers, 'The Meaning of Development', in *International Development Review* 11(4) 1969)

In other words, merely to analyse statistics of industrial output or the levels of manufacturing capacity is to miss, perhaps conveniently, a number of very important points: for example, (1) that such industrialisation may well be *capital intensive* with a correspondingly low level of effect upon employment within the national labour force; and, (2) that such 'industrialisation' may take the form of mere '*assembly points*' where high-technology components produced in the developed countries are put together using relatively low-level industrial technology (with commensurately low-level industrial wages and conditions). The real effect of these conditions is to produce an illusory picture of 'independent' progress towards industrialisation which masks the true state of affairs.

Further, the idea that it is possible to compare the rate of industrial growth and output within capitalist countries with those of the Third World can be said to be misleading. This is because there are fundamental differences in forms of industrial organisation. For example, in Third World industrial operations workers are generally not shielded by the legislation which protects the pay and conditions of their First World counterparts. Gunder Frank has shown conclusively the wide differentials which exist:

In Hong Kong work weeks of over sixty hours are common. Indeed, the Hong Kong Trade Development Council itself advertises that 'there is no legal restriction on the hours of work for men over the age of 18 years. Consequently many men work ten hours a day, with a rest period of one or two hours, although three shift working, enabling machinery to be used 24 hours a day is common' . . . According to the 1971 census, 174,439 workers worked 75 hours a week or more . . . the greatest extension of the economy-wide work week is in South Korea, which is a 'model' of export promotion. There seven-day, eighty-four-hour work weeks are not uncommon, and sixty-hour work weeks are normal.

(André Gunder Frank, *Crisis: in the Third World*, Heinemann, 1981, pp. 169–70)

Critical examination of the wider impact on national development has shown the existence of what amounts to a consolidated network of power radiating from the centres of developed nations. This has, in the view of dependency analysts, produced a system of global stratification between nations similar to that seen between individuals living under conditions of industrial capitalism. It is precisely this gross structured inequality that the critics of functionalist/modernisation theory have attempted to highlight in their work.

2 Can there be post-industrialisation independence for the Third World?

Warren's analysis of the experience of the emerging Third World nations upon the pathway towards industrialisation is intended to show how, once the seeds have been sown, there can develop a '*free-standing*' national economy. In evidence, Warren points to the great strides taken by many Third World countries towards nationalisation, whereby control is taken over by indigenous groups using quite sophisticated technological and production methods. In the world markets, therefore, according to Warren's thesis, many of the developing nations trade as independent units free from the controls of the aiding nations.

Warren's arguments have been the subject of much critical scrutiny; his table of the fastest-growing 'independent nations' has been challenged by P. McMichael, J. Petras, and R. Rhodes (*New Left Review* 85, May–June 1974) on the grounds that if, as he suggests, their industrial growth was occurring in a *truly* independent manner, then the most successful of such nations may be expected to show an increased success in reducing their financial indebtedness to the international capitalist world. In reality, as Warren's critics have shown, using figures from the *International Bank for Reconstruction and Development Report*, exactly the opposite seems to be happening (see Figure 6.1).

Thus, although superficially it may appear as if a picture of true independence and growing equality of status between the developed and developing industrialised nations emerges, the actual situation is one in which *financial* dependency becomes ever more firmly entrenched. It is the gigantic multinationals, together with the vast capital reservoirs of the International Monetary Fund and

Figure 6.1 **External public debt outstanding 31 December 1971**

	Total	Per capita	Service payments as % of exports 1965	1971
Philippines	960.2	25.32	5.4	7.0
Singapore	301.5	142.90	0.1	0.7
Pakistan	4,613.9	36.40	11.8	21.6
Turkey	2,981.7	82.57	20.3	19.4
Brazil	5,236.2	54.50	20.9	17.1
Costa Rica	233.8	131.61	10.3	9.9
Mexico	4,243.7	83.49	24.8	24.7
Peru	1,239.1	88.44	7.0	19.4

Source: *International Bank for Reconstruction and Development Report*, 1972–73, Tables 5 and 6, and United Nations population statistics quoted in 'Imperialism and the contradictions of development', P. McMichael, J. Petras and R. Rhodes, in *New Left Review* 85, May/June 1974, 96

the World Bank, which retain the economic, political and social controls upon the developing societies. This covert control, as Teresa Hayter has remarked, has the following results: 'gross inflows of official and private capital are now exceeded by gross outflows of profits, repatriated and expatriated capital, repayments and interest' (T. Hayter, *Aid as Imperialism*, Penguin, 1971, p. 173).

The granting of 'independence' is presented to the world as a philanthropic gesture by the 'benefactor' state giving 'freedom' to a previously subject people. It may, however, also be seen as the creation of a cynical illusion whereby control is maintained without the necessity of military or legal intervention from outside the newly 'independent' state.

The result of this process is that the previous colonialist social organisation continues to operate as before, though in a covert manner. In this way, markets are maintained and expanded for the sale of a multitude of items produced within the high-tech industries of the developed nations; goods such as hi-fi, television sets, videos, electronic calculators, computers and so on. Other consumer goods are, through massive advertising campaigns,

Figure 6.2
Ex-colonial powers and governments of countries with substantial interests in Third World nations frequently install and maintain in power political groups sympathetic to their ideology. Many examples of this process can be given; Claudia Wright, for example, has indicated the US record in this area of activity. In an article entitled 'It's Business as Usual with "Friendly" Despots', she writes:

IN THE LAST [sic] five months, the US has intervened in attempts to replace formerly close allies: Samuel Doe in Liberia, Jean-Claude Duvalier in Haiti and now Ferdinand Marcos in the Philippines. . . . The President still believes, in Jeanne Kirkpatrick's words, that 'the fabric of authority unravels quickly when the power and status of the man at the top are undermined or eliminated'. What this means in practice is that the US will not cut down a friendly dictator unless Washington has full control over his successor. . . . In Haiti, for most of last year Ambassador Clayton McManaway regularly met US researchers throughout the island before deciding there was an alternative to Duvalier that would preserve US control of Haiti – indeed enhance US popularity by eliminating the Duvalier abuses. This alternative was the military junta headed by General Henri Namphy that seized power on 7 February, with an army and civil bureaucracy whose salaries are paid out of US funds. The result was one that brought cheerful US flag-wavers on to the streets of Port-au-Prince and added to the Administration's confidence that it can 'restore' democracy without damaging strategic interests.
    (*New Statesman*, 21 Feb. 1986, 17–18)

The USA has also intervened in the ex-colonial interests of one of its own allies – the United Kingdom. Grenada, a former British colony in the Windward Islands, was the subject of an attempted socialist revolution. This was uncomfortably close to 'America's own back-yard', and it was with all speed that the US responded to the organisation of East Caribbean states' request for help. Peter Pringle

('Deserted Island', *New Statesman*, 11 Nov. 1983), described the events in the following words:

> the Grenadians . . . were obviously stunned by the sheer force of the invasion: 5,000 men (one for every 20 Grenadians); the sky dotted permanently with noisy helicopters and even noisier fighter bombers; the tiny roads clogged with soldiers, jeeps and trucks; the infamous British and Cuban-built 9,000-foot runway at Point Salines cluttered with C-130 transports.. . . Washington has done its damnedest to make sure that a socialist Grenada got no foreign aid at all; or that, when elections are held next year, it may not approve of the new Government. It might not be the 'suitable' administration that Major Douglas Frey, of the 82nd Airborne, told journalists was what the American troops had come to install.

shown to be of a highly desirable nature; products such as Coca-Cola and many harmful tobacco products (which are becoming increasingly difficult to sell in the developed world) sell in increasing quantities throughout the Third World.

In order to pay for such luxury consumer goods which the people of the Third World are encouraged to buy, they are encouraged to find work within the large multinational organisations. So, in today's system of relations between developed and developing societies, the previous 'cash-crop' economy is largely replaced by a 'manufacturing' economy in which the poorer nations become assembly shops supplying cheap labour producing hi-tech goods for sale in the Western economies. Examine, if you will, the country of origin of most mass-consumption clothing, electrical/electronic equipment, cameras, and so on, which are available in the large department stores of the affluent Western industrialised nations.

The economic features of the relationships between the developed world and the underdeveloped nations are further discussed in the next chapter. It must also be noted, however, that there is a political dimension to the international system of structured inequality which exists. The advanced industrial nations continually struggle to retain their influence in the developing world in order to protect their own particular dominant values. In an interesting article, Claudia Wright has explained why the United States became involved in the internal affairs of Somalia:

THERE IS A JOKE [sic] circulating in Mogadishu, the capital of Somalia in the Horn of Africa. Mohammed Siad Barre, the President of Somalia since 1969, is the first dictator in the world to be run over by a bus. Few Somalis would shed tears over the man who precipitated Somalia's catastrophic defeat in the 1977 war with Ethiopia over the Ogaden region; who abruptly switched foreign protectors by evicting the Soviets and inviting the Americans and (more recently) the South Africans to take their place; and who has escalated his differences with his critics and political opponents into a ruinous and bitter civil war that is still being fought in the northern half of the country. . . . For the Reagan administration there is much at stake. Its allies in the neighbouring governments of the Sudan and Egypt are under serious political challenge at home, and might lose their nerve altogether if the Americans were to lose their grip on Somalia. They need reassurance. The CIA is busy at a variety of covert operations to weaken, and if possible topple, the Ethiopian regime. The director of Central Intelligence, William Casey, dreams of avenging past losses and humiliations in the Horn of Africa, and of returning the region to the Anglo-American protectorate as it was in the days of Emperor Haile Selassie. And then there is the agreement Siad Barre signed to allow the US military use of Berbera, the strategically located port on guard at the entrance to the Red Sea and Suez Canal, across the water from the Saudi Kingdom, and within striking distance of the Soviet bases in Southern Yemen.

('Holding a Neo-colony', *New Statesman*, 6 June 1986, 19–20)

7 Development as exploitation: the development of underdevelopment

In the previous chapter we have seen how, in his development of the work of Karl Marx, Lenin altered the focus of the analysis of social change to emphasise the international dimension. In the process of doing this he laid the foundation for further analyses of the relations between advanced industrial nations and the developing world. More specifically, these relations are viewed as not merely dependency-inducing, but also as a form of systematic and structured (though frequently covert) exploitation through the medium of international finance capital.

A number of modern analysts have sought further to extend the analysis of international capitalist relations in order to identify their role in Third World underdevelopment and global deprivation. One such analyst is the eminent academic André Gunder Frank, whose title to Chapter 1 of his work *Latin America: Underdevelopment or Revolution* forms the subtitle to this present chapter.

Frank's approach to the analysis of international relations is based upon a historical view which he sees as recording the tendency for capitalism always to overwhelm and transform traditional economic and cultural systems. Once capitalist intervention is made in a society, Frank has observed, there comes into existence a two-tier economic system in which the centres of capitalism – large cities – begin to extract wealth from the poorer hinterland through patterns of unequal 'trading' without materially doing anything to increase the wealth of the 'host' society generally. The result is that the already relatively poor country becomes more impoverished due to the removal of its natural resources and wealth through the exploitative effects of these urban centres of capitalism. As another analyst of the process remarked,

> the line of demarcation between big business and the village is sometimes so sharp that the western enterprise appears like a capitalist enclave in a foreign land . . . the whole concern is

detached from its surroundings, although its indirect influence
on these surroundings is penetrating.
(J. Boeke, *Economics and Economic Policy of Dual Societies*,
New York: Institute of Pacific Relations, 1953, p. 103)

In his first book, *Capitalism and Underdevelopment in Latin
America*, Gunder Frank proposed as his main thesis that Third
World underdevelopment is the result of deliberate and systematic
exploitation through the market forces of capitalism on a global
scale. He went on to assert that only in gaining true independence
by removing the international 'master – servant' relationship can
the Third World nations ever hope to achieve true social
development.

It is not, however, only the system of social and economic
relations between nations of which Frank is highly critical. He has
claimed that the sociology carried out in the developed countries,
especially in the USA, is inadequate satisfactorily to address the
central issues involved in the analysis of international capitalist
relations. He has asserted that

On critical examination, this new sociology of development is
found to be empirically invalid when confronted with reality,
theoretically inadequate in terms of its own classical social
scientific standards, and policy-wise ineffective for pursuing its
supposed intentions of promoting the development of the
underdeveloped countries . . . Like the underdeveloped society
to which it is applied, this sociology is becoming increasingly
underdeveloped.
(A. G. Frank, *Economics and Economic Policy of Dual Societies*,
p. 21)

Frank has made a plea for the production of a sociological
perspective which will enable an analysis of the fundamental issues
in social development satisfactorily to be carried out. In his view,
most sociology in the developed nations has largely ignored the
exploitative nature of capitalist market relations between developed and underdeveloped nations. Further, he has implied that
this is really not surprising since the rationale underlying much
of the sociology produced in the developed world is political
rather than sociological; that is to say that its function appears to
be to lay an effective smoke-screen of intellectualism over the
true, exploitative nature of international affairs.

In a more recent work (*Crisis: In the Third World*, Heinemann, 1981), Frank has identified a further element in the relations between poor and rich nations. This element he termed 'super-exploitation' – a condition which he has described as a process in which workers in Third World countries are paid very low wages for working very long hours producing consumer goods for export to the affluent nations. The workers are kept in control by the governing elite of the Third World nations themselves, since these officials are well paid by, and so highly supportive of, developed governments and multinational companies. In addition, the old system of pre-capitalist exploitative relations – landlord and peasant – are ideally suited to the style of capitalist relations. Baran has described the situation clearly:

> the age-old exploitation of the population of underdeveloped countries by their domestic overlords was freed of the mitigating constraints inherited from the feudal tradition. This superimposition of business mores over ancient oppression by landed gentries resulted in compounded exploitation, more outrageous corruption, and more glaring injustice.
> (P. Baran, 'On the Political Economy of Backwardness', in *Imperialism and Underdevelopment: a Reader*, R. I. Rhodes (ed.), Monthly Review Press, 1970, p. 286)

Thus, the overriding feature governing relations between rich and poor is, in the view of Frank and many other commentators, the relentless pursuit of profit irrespective of any moral constraints which may superficially be thought to apply. The support given by governments of Western industrial nations to many dictatorial, near-fascist, regimes throughout the world appears effectively to underline such a point of view, and the conclusion may be drawn that, under capitalism, profit takes precedence over human rights or the democratic process (see Figure 7.1).

Gunder Frank's view of underdevelopment being the result of structured, systematic and deliberate policies of exploitation finds support in the work of two other analysts, Baran and Sweezy, who, after extensive analysis of modern monopoly capitalism, have concluded 'that foreign investment, far from being an outlet for domestically generated surplus, is a most efficient device for transferring surplus generated abroad to the investing country' (P. A. Baran and P. M. Sweezy, *Monopoly Capital*, Penguin, 1973, p. 113).

Figure 7.1 **People . . . or Profit?**

Britain has consistently refused to stop the sale of armaments to the white South African regime in spite of a United Nations embargo on the sale of weapons to a country where 4 million whites dictate the life style of over 20 million black people who are not permitted to vote. The disenfranchised black population makes up 80 per cent of the population of South Africa, yet they are only allowed to live in 13 per cent of the land area of their own country. A UN motion of censure condemning the South African government was vetoed by the British government, thereby, in effect, declaring approval by the British government of the conditions existing in that country.

Again, Britain continued with the sale of armaments to the fascist regime of General Galtieri in Argentina until the outbreak of the Falklands War. It is little comfort to those casualties of that war to know that they were, possibly, injured by the products of the British armaments industry. Political as well as economic reasons may also be seen to prevail in the United States support for right-wing forces (Contras) in Nicaragua as they try to remove the first democratically elected government in the history of that country. (The Sandinistas won 66.7 per cent of the vote; 61 out of the 96 seats in the National Assembly.) Of the situation in Nicaragua, John Pilger has written:

> President Reagan has described the Contras as 'our brothers' and 'the moral equal of our Founding Fathers'. Documentation shows that between 1982 and 1985 Contra death squads have murdered 3346 children and teenagers and killed one or both parents of 6236 children. During one year, 1984, the Contras caused an average of more than four deaths every day. At President Reagan's tireless urging – Nicaragua is said to be 'his' issue – the US Congress in October, 1986 approved 100 million dollars in military aid to the Contras. Allegations emerging from the 'Irangate' scandal estimate that a further 30 million dollars were illegally diverted to the Contras from the sale of arms to Iran. . . .

> When Reagan commands headlines around the world by describing Nicaragua as 'the new version of Murder Incorporated', a country which gives a 'haven to the IRA' and whose 'acts of war against the United States' justify US military action to defend itself, some may feel an uncomfortable urge to laugh at such apparent disingenuousness. But that would be to miss the point. 'So obsessed is the Reagan administration', wrote Charles Maechling from Washington, '. . . that it has not hesitated to twist through redefinition the meaning of human rights in order to downgrade the most basic right of all, the right to life. Its acquiescence in patterns of torture, murder and other forms of state terrorism . . . comes close to condoning the kind of crimes against humanity condemned at the Nuremberg war crimes trials.'
> (J. Pilger, *Heroes*, Pan Books, 1986, p. 472)

Such a view is in direct opposition to that of the modernisation theorists who, it may be remembered, see financial capital as a catalyst to economic growth in the Third World; a form of international 'enterprise scheme' enabling the less developed nations to become economically viable international units in their own right. These investments, be they as 'loans' or as 'aid', seem, in reality, to have only one aim, which is the maximum return of profit to the government or multinational company making the investment.

This view is apparently confirmed by another writer, Teresa Hayter, who, as a member of the staff of the Overseas Development Institute, was commissioned by the World Bank to study the true nature of the relationships between aid donors and the recipient nations. What she discovered led the World Bank to dismiss both her and her findings, for, contrary to their expectations, Hayter found that what was deemed to be 'aid' – by implication a voluntary donation from the affluent nations – was, in reality, nothing short of a loan with a number of strings attached to it. As she has pointed out:

Aid is, in general, available to countries whose internal political arrangements, foreign policy alignments, treatment of foreign private investment, debt-servicing record, export policies and so on, are considered desirable, potentially desirable, or at least acceptable, to the countries or institutions providing aid, and which do not appear to threaten their interests. . . . Supporters of aid argue that promoting economic development in poor countries is in the long-term interests of the developed countries.

(T. Hayter, *Aid as Imperialism*, Penguin, 1971, pp. 15–16)

President Kennedy of the United States once made a similar point in relation to the granting of aid to developing countries when he stated that 'Foreign aid is a method by which the United States maintains a position of influence and control around the world' (quoted by R. B. Sutcliffe, in *The Political Economy of Growth*, by P. Baran, Penguin, 1973, p. 81). This attitude appears to be enshrined in the philosophy of US institutions, especially the one known by the acronym AID (Agency for International Development), for, in a document entitled 'Principles of Foreign Economic Assistance', three criteria are set out for the guidance of those involved in the granting of aid to developing countries:

1 the effectiveness with which the country can use available resources – both internal and external – to promote the economic growth of the country;
2 the importance to the United States of sustaining or accelerating the economic growth of that country;
3 the availability to the country of other external resources in a suitable form.

(Quoted in Hayter, *Aid as Imperialism*, pp. 87–8)

In general terms there appears to be a mismatch between the official proclamations made by the governments of nations giving 'aid' to the developing nations and the practical effects of their actions. Perhaps a more realistic view of the relationship between capitalist enterprise and government policy to be found in capitalist nations may be obtained from the view of the historian W. A. Williams, who claimed that 'it was the need for American corporations to expand their investments and protect their markets that led to such diverse developments as the US involvement in Vietnam, the Marshall Plan to aid Western Europe and American intervention against the left-wing regime of Salvador Allende in Chile' (*US News and World Report*, 25 January 1982, 6).

The analytical perspective which has been a consistent theme of Frank's work is seen, by many writers of a classical Marxist and neo-Marxist persuasion, to be fundamentally flawed. A major criticism levelled against his work is that, by equating trading relationships or exchange of commodities with capitalism, he has made a fundamental error of definition.

Critiques of Frank

In 1971, Ernesto Laclau publicly took issue with Frank in an article entitled 'Feudalism and Capitalism in Latin America' (*New Left Review* 67, May/June 1971, 19–37). Laclau stressed the importance of the conditions of production over the conditions of exchange. This he did by establishing a definition of a mode of production which comprised four parts: the pattern of ownership of the means of production; the degree to which division of labour had occurred; the level of development of the forces of production; and the way in which what he calls 'economic surplus' (profit) is distributed. It is clear that Laclau agreed with Frank's view of capitalism as an international system, but he went on to point out that it is erroneous to assume that this implies uniformity of mode of production. Within the global capitalist system there are, Laclau declared, a wide range of different modes of production. This is to say that both capitalist and non-capitalist modes of production can, and do, coexist, albeit with the capitalist mode of production in a pre-eminent position. To try and apply one all-enveloping theoretical model to this range of social relations in terms of Frank's view of an homogeneous capitalist system is, for Laclau, grossly to oversimplify a highly complex situation.

Laclau's critique was significant in pointing out the direction of future analysis of development from the dependency perspective. The main objective of Marxist analysts of development became an attempt to analyse underdevelopment in terms of relationships between capitalist and non-capitalist modes of production instead of Frank's one-sided accentuation of market forces. One way in which capitalist and non-capitalist modes of production may be seen to be combined has been provided by J. G. Taylor (*From Modernisation to Modes of Production: a Critique of the Sociologies of Development and Underdevelopment*, Macmillan,

1979). Taylor has carried Laclau's scheme further by making the suggestion that societies within the Third World should be analysed in terms of the total impact of introducing capitalism into pre-capitalist societies. He has also noted that such a situation produces a condition in which the modes of production coexist in a strictly independent fashion. Capitalism is almost always in a dominant position, and this brings about what Boeke (*Economics and Economic Policy of Dual Societies*, Institute of Pacific Relations, 1953) has termed 'dual societies'. Celseo Furtado has described such an effect of capitalist intervention in South America:

> The economic structure of the region into which the capitalist enterprise has penetrated does not necessarily become modified as a result of that penetration . . . displacement of the European frontier almost always resulted in the formation of hybrid economies in which a capitalist nucleus, so to speak, existed in a state of 'peaceful coexistence' with an archaic structure.
> ('Elements of a Theory of Underdevelopment', in *Underdevelopment and Development*, H. Bernstein (ed.), Penguin, 1973, pp. 35–6)

Thus, within the Third World nations, a 'capitalist nucleus' forms in the larger towns and city centres of commerce which is largely separate from the agrarian hinterland. A further complication of the situation occurs due to the subdivision of this urban capitalist class into two main groups. On the one hand there are those who operate as paid agents of overseas capitalists (known as 'compradors'); while on the other there are those whose economic interests lie in the unilateral development of the domestic economy ('nationalist' bourgeoisie).

In the opinion of another analyst, the divergence of allegiance between the compradors and the nationalist capitalists severely weakens the power of the bourgeoisie in Third World societies (I. Roxborough, *Theories of Underdevelopment*, Macmillan, 1979). He has pointed out that because the bourgeoisie lack a unity of purpose they cannot operate effectively as a significant force for change. This means that they cannot, therefore, take the leading role which, historically, the bourgeoisie played in the Western society's transformation from an agrarian to an industrial form of socio-economic organisation.

Another approach which arose in response to the dialogue between Frank and Laclau deserves attention here. This analytical approach assumes that the capitalist mode of production is in a dominant position throughout the world economy. In other words, the basis of the world economy is seen to be capitalist in orientation, and, therefore, development throughout the world will tend to be subject to the effect of that particular mode of production. The emphasis of 'world capitalism' theorists is upon a global analysis of capitalist production, which is viewed as a combination of both circulation (that is, trading and exchange, as in Frank) and of production (as in Laclau). The international feature which is seen as representative of this international capitalist system of accumulation is the multinational companies. However, the world capitalism theorists formulate differing interpretations in answer to questions relating to the nature of the relationship between dependency and underdevelopment.

First, there are those theorists who claim that the internationalisation of capital has produced a global division of labour which serves to maintain the dependency of the underdeveloped nations upon the nations in which the multinational companies have their headquarters (F. Frobe, J. Heinrichs, and O. Kreye, *The New International Division of Labour: Structural Unemployment in Industrialised Countries and Industrialisation in Developing Countries*, CUP, 1981).

Second, there are those who argue that the spread of capitalism throughout the world has produced a process of capitalist development in all parts of underdeveloped societies. The state of underdevelopment is seen from this aspect as resulting from a continuation of the non-capitalist modes of production. Once capitalism has been embraced by the underdeveloped society, then, according to these theorists, the stage is set not only for economic growth (development), but also for *independent* development (B. Warren, *Imperialism: Pioneer of Capitalism*, New Left Books, 1980; see also J. M. Cypher, 'The Internationalization of Capital and the Transformation of Social Formations: Critique of the *Monthly Review* School', *Review of Radical Political Economics* 11, Winter 1979, 33–49).

These criticisms of Frank's work seem to imply that a full analysis of Third World poverty and the reasons for it requires a more complex conceptual framework within which to operate. In recent years there has emerged a tentative movement towards synthesis of aspects of both the developmentalist and the dependency approaches. Such an approach has, as its basis, a notion of the role of the state as the initiator of economic growth within any society. Some writers of a Marxist and neo-Marxist persuasion have suggested that greater credence should be given to the internal aspects of societies undergoing development. Additionally, there are writers of a developmentalist character who have moved away significantly from the principles of *laissez-faire* in order to propose that the state has a quite specific contribution to make in the development of Third World economies.

PART 3

The limitations of developmentalist and dependency theories

8 Development strategies

One of the most significant features of advanced industrial societies is the degree to which they have achieved progress in the fields of science and technology. In large measure this has enabled them to achieve economic primacy and has ensured that their citizens enjoy a material standard of living which far exceeds that of the Third World. The contrast between the industrial and non-industrial societies could scarcely be greater. Indeed, the level of deprivation which is a feature of daily life for the overwhelming majority of people in underdeveloped countries is rarely seen, even in isolated cases, in the affluent nations; famine and disease of a level to be seen today in the Third World is virtually unthinkable. In order to enable the underdeveloped to 'catch up' with the more advanced societies, modernisation theorists have, as we have seen, put forward the proposition that it is necessary to install the characteristics of industrial society in the poor countries. In this way it is thought that wealth may be generated which could rapidly effect the transition from poverty to relative affluence.

In the first section of this part of the book we will examine the effects of modernisation procedure in the light of actual events through the examination, in a very generalised way, of the fortunes of India. By an inquiry into the assumptions implicit in developmentalism – that is, that the advanced societies represent an 'ideal-type' role model for Third World nations, characteristics of which may be introduced into individual societies – it is hoped to note the limitations of developmentalist theory as an explanatory paradigm, and also of its ideological expression, modernisation, as a process in effecting development.

CASE STUDY: DEVELOPMENTALIST/MODERNISATION
THEORY – INDIA

Before being colonised, India was governed by a ruling minority called Moguls. These people were the descendants of followers of Baber who conquered the country in the fifteenth century. The 'Mogul economy', as it became known, continued until the Indian Mutiny of 1857, when effective control of India passed into the hands of the British Crown.

It has been argued that, economically, India was quite prosperous under the Mogul economy, especially in the eighteenth century when, according to one Indian historian, the country became 'a great manufacturing as well as a great agricultural country' (R. C. Dutt, *The Economic History of India 1757–1837*, Delhi: Government of India reprint, 1963, p. xxv). The system of government was fierce and repressive, for the Moguls were warlords and held tight controls over their lands, yet, for all that, it was quite complex with a sophisticated hierarchy (caste system) and fiscal (taxation) policy. The system of taxation was heavily reliant upon the taxation of land, with the main aim appearing to have been the extraction of the greatest tax payment by the villagers to the Mogul minority. The effect of this repressive system, however, was retrogressive, since it inhibited the growth of production and generation of capital by consistently reducing the standard of living of the peasant groups. In turn, this considerably reduced both their ability and motivation to work effectively; a situation which resulted in continual low production.

On 10 May 1858 the Bengal Army mutinied against what they saw as the attempted reforms of Indian traditional institutions by the British. The sepoys (soldiers employed by the British) refused to obey orders from British officers at Meerut. The subsequent murder of the officers signalled the beginning of a fierce sepoy rebellion. Basically, they objected because of their fear of enforced conversion to the Christian faith and the issue of cartridges coated in beef fat (offensive to the Hindus), or pig fat (offensive to the Muslims). Three regiments marched upon Delhi, where Bahadur Shah was installed as Emperor by the rebellious troops. Others marched upon Lucknow, and, for a period of many weeks, appalling atrocities were perpetrated, with many thousands of people being killed. After extensive, and bloody, fighting, the British regained control of India on 8 July 1858. In August of that same year, the British government proclaimed the India Act which effected the transfer of power in India from the East India Company to the British monarch. So began the period of British rule in India which was to last until Indian independence was granted at midnight on 14–15 August 1947.

The main motive behind British involvement in India was the achievement of a monopoly of trade. Investments by British people increased dramatically, doubtless attracted by the enormous level of return on capital which was to be made. Indeed, so great was the amount yielded in profit that the British in India were able to make sizeable contributions to the British balance of payments (A. Maddison, *Class Structure and Economic Growth*, George Allen & Unwin, 1971, p. 35).

Colonial rule had, however, other very important effects in that the internal social organisation of India was significantly altered. For example, the old Mogul ruling aristocracy was replaced by a bureaucratic administration which was reinforced in authority by a powerful, modern militia. All of this was paid for by funds from taxation which had previously been used by the Moguls to finance their own extravagant life style. The top echelon of the Indian social scale was severely abbreviated with only relatively few of the Mogul princes being retained, for reasons of expediency, by the British colonisers.

The officers of the new bureaucracy set about the modernisation of the Indian economic system after the style of that in Britain. What this did was to effect increases in industrial output and in level of trading, with both of these sectors of the economy becoming almost totally reliant upon British management. In broad terms it may be said that, bureaucrats apart, there was very little transfer of modern industrial, managerial and commercial skill from British to Indian personnel. As a result, while the economy of India grew together with its population, there was little or no change in the level of income per head amongst the indigenous population, and the overall level of industrialisation was inhibited 'to make India subservient to the Industries of Great Britain, and to make the Indian people grow raw produce only, in order to supply material for the looms and manufactories of Great Britain' (Dutt, *The Economic History of India 1757–1837*, ibid.). This restriction of industrial growth by the British vested interests was claimed by Jawaharlal Nehru, India's first Prime Minister and Minister of Foreign Affairs after independence in 1947, to have been 'the real fundamental cause of the appalling poverty of the Indian people' (J. Nehru, *The Discovery of India*, Day, 1946, p. 299).

India was granted independence from British colonial rule in 1947 amid great pomp and ceremony. What had been a complex and uneasy mixture of traditional values with an alien culture now embarked upon the difficult process of becoming a coherent nation with its own identity. Western influence or, more especially, British interests did not suddenly come to an end at this point, however. This was because the ideological commitment of the colonisers remained effectively socialised in the officers whose task was to continue the operation of the bureaucratic system of government.

Since independence there has been consistent growth of the Indian economy, undoubtedly helped by the fact that the bureaucracy has effectively carried on the role of a modernising force. Indeed, the administrative and military sector has significantly increased in size and influence through successive governments, with an ever-increasing difference between the income levels in urban-industrial and rural life. In very general terms it is possible to identify an urban-based industrial/governing bureaucratic elite whose life style is quite comfortable, or even opulent, living amongst a large mass of extremely deprived people existing in filth and squalor. Further, in rural areas there are village capitalist landlords who, through the caste system of stratification, still retain a relatively wealthy life style at the expense of the virtually destitute and enslaved peasant masses.

Because of the availability of cheap and plentiful labour many Western industrial enterprises, with the direct help of indigenous capitalists and bureaucrats, have continued the process of installing increasingly high-technology processes into the Indian economy. None other than Rajiv Gandhi, the present Prime Minister, said recently that India must make rapid progress in both industrial and technological fields in order to compensate for more than three hundred years which have been lost. With such powerful advocates for modernisation, it is scarcely surprising to find that the level of modernisation in contemporary India is very great — at least in certain key economic areas. This does, however, pose significant problems when seen in the context of the society as a whole. As S. K. Goyal of New Delhi University has pointed out, there is an 'unfortunate assumption . . . that when technology arrives here, it is transferred. We are finding that the technology often just gets transferred to the premises of the subsidiary, not into the society as a whole. It stays within the walls of the factory' (quoted in A. Harrigan, 'The Limits of Modernization', *Contemporary Review* 249, 113). Goyal was commenting after the horrific accident at the Union Carbide plant in Bhopal, where vast quantities of deadly gas escaped from a highly complex industrial chemical plant built in the centre of a city filled with a population whose world horizons were bounded by their experience of agrarian society. To them the plant was virtually incomprehensible, and so they were oblivious to the dangers of having such a unit in their midst. Further, those employed in the plant were 'recruited from the agricultural age that is India in the main today. Their minds were still back in that age, though the plan was predicated on the employment of people from the technological age' (Harrigan, ibid.).

There is currently a growing awareness of the pitfalls which are to be found in modernisation as a way of 'progress'. This awareness is growing amongst the intellectuals of the developing societies and is beginning to stimulate a fundamental questioning of this particular path to economic progress. In 1988, a meeting of the Society for International Development was told that, in India, the main obstacle to development is the middle class. The speaker was Rajni Kothari, the head of a group concerned with effecting a stop to modernisationist development. This group, called Lokayan, has emphatically rejected the notion of 'Third Worldism' together with the attendant emphasis of 'catching up' with the industrialised Western and Eastern bloc countries. One Lokayan member, Professor Dhirubhai Seth, has set out demands for what he sees as a 'fourth type of society that must arise from the untouchables of development' (quoted in W. Schwarz, 'The Menace of Development', *The Guardian*, 20 June 1988, 19).

Thus it may be seen that modernisationist development is doing little to effect significant changes in the basic structure of the Indian economy. Certainly, there is affluence being generated, but this is distributed only amongst the few urban and rural middle classes who retain their profit-making as a sort of cartel. For the vast majority of the already impoverished population the future is far from becoming rosy or in any way comforting. International 'modernisation' intervention, either by direct capital investment or through so-called 'aid' programmes, enables the already established controlling group to entrench their position of dominance even more firmly.

Due to observable reality falling rather short of the forecasts made by the developmentalists, the debate over developmental process shifted from concern with the microstructural, internal aspects of individual nations to focus upon the macrostructural, external features of development (or apparent lack of it) in the Third World. This change of focus examines the system of international capitalism and its role in Third World poverty. A central feature is the rejection of the modernist view of an industrialised 'ideal-type' which may be followed by impoverished societies. On the contrary, this poverty is seen as the direct consequence of the affluence of the advanced societies. As Griffin has remarked, 'Europe did not "discover" the underdeveloped countries; on the contrary, she created them' (K. Griffin, 'Underdevelopment in History', in C. K. Wilber (ed.) *The Economy of Development and Underdeveloped*, Random House, 1973). In a more forthright manner, Fanon has summed up the general view of dependency theorists in the following terms: 'The well-being and the progress of Europe have been built up with the sweat and the dead bodies of Negroes, Arabs, Indians and the yellow races' (F. Fanon, *The Wretched of the Earth*, Penguin, 1974, p. 76).

How far does this explanatory paradigm agree with reality? In order to test this, the experiences of another Third World country – South Korea – will be examined in general terms of its political and economic history, a brief summary of which now follows.

CASE STUDY: DEPENDENCY THEORIES – THE REPUBLIC OF SOUTH KOREA
Korea was a united entity in the seventeenth century when, in 1637, it was conquered and taken into the control of the Chinese Emperor. Because of its geographical location, jutting out into the Sea of Japan between China to the north and west and Japan to the east, Korea has been consistently the subject of rival powers. In the closing years of the nineteenth century, China and Japan went to war over Korea. This resulted in the establishment of Korea as an independent nation through the Treaty of Shimonoseki, which was signed on 17 April 1895 between China and Japan, with China agreeing to pay significant reparation to Japan as well as yielding advantageous commercial rights. In spite of

powerful international diplomacy by France, Russia and Germany to try and limit the claims of Japan upon the territory, Japan's influence in the area remained relatively high as it effectively retained its economic and political domination.

Around the turn of the twentieth century (1898–1904) the Russians embarked upon a series of incursions into the north of Korea with the aim of establishing trading connections along the length of the Yalu river. These commercial transactions were not tolerated by the Japanese, who viewed them as a significant threat to their economic penetration of both Korea and Manchuria. On 8 February 1904, the Japanese attacked the Russian Navy without formally declaring war. What resulted was a war between Russia and Japan which ended in September 1906 with the United States acting as mediator. Japan had effectively beaten off the Russian challenge and, from November 1905, took over effective control of Korea with total annexation of the country following in August 1910. This signalled the beginning of an influx of Japanese settlers into Korea, especially around the region of Seoul, who gradually established themselves as an economic and political elite.

Towards the end of the Second World War, Russian forces again entered Korea in the north and gained a significant foothold in that area. American interests were concentrated in the eastern half of the country as a result of the conquest of Japan by the US forces following the Second World War. Such a situation, in which two opposing ideologies were competing for control of the same area, generated continu.   ggravation which culminated in the outbreak of the Korean War in June 1950. The forces of the United Nations were deployed in support of the South Koreans, while those of the Soviet Union and the Republic of China went to the assistance of the North Koreans. After many bloody battles, peace was declared in July 1953, and hesitant agreement was reached to divide the country along a line roughly along the 38th parallel. This division meant that most of the extractive industry and heavy industrial plant was in the hands of the Russian-controlled north, the American-controlled south having only relatively light industrialisation with a preponderance of agriculture (mainly paddy fields for rice production).

The costs of this war were immense to all concerned. Over 1 million died, with many times this figure injured and destitute. This level of human misery was compounded by the virtual decimation of the economy, and the country was maintained only by the injection of American military and capital resources. Such investment, following the modernisationist ideology, was accompanied by stringent controls and effective intervention in the internal dynamics of the country. The rigorous nature of the controlling regime, together with powerful protectionist policies (designed to discourage imports), ensured that industrial output grew at a rapid pace and that there was an accent upon the need to export.

A military dictatorship under General (later President) Park followed the removal of President Synghman Rhee from office through a *coup d'état* in 1960. This regime continued the repressive control of the country and increased the emphasis upon exporting in order to achieve economic growth. The overt involvement of the United States' investments was gradually wound down and the Korean economy seemed set to justify the advocates of modernisation and the *laissez-faire* economists. In 1973 the Korean regime implemented the Heavy Industry and Chemicals plan which set out to increase the emphasis of production in these areas irrespective of the cost in human terms. These costs were recognised by no less an authority than the US Congress when, in April 1978, it noted that

> At the heart of Korea's human rights problems is the economic growth strategy of the country, a strategy which requires the repression and manipulation of labour (through government-controlled 'trade unions' and a ban on strikes) and the tight control of free political expression.
>
> (Quoted in A. G. Frank, *Crisis in the Third World*, Heinemann Educational Books, p. 190).

The severe repression of the dictatorial regime was temporarily suspended by the murder, in October 1979, of President Park. In 1981 the ensuing government embarked upon a series of economic reforms at the behest of the World Bank and the International Monetary Fund to whom they had turned for assistance and advice. This is not to say that foreign investment was increased; on the contrary, as Nigel Harris has pointed out, 'South Korea is not a notable recipient of foreign investment. . . . Furthermore, foreign investment followed accelerated growth rather than leading it. . . . The great transnationals were rather remote in such a context' (*The End of the Third World*, Penguin, 1987, p. 45).

Thus it would appear that in the case of South Korea an initial impetus towards economic development resulted in a major step forward by that country almost unilaterally. Since that time, Korea has been co-opted into the world trading system and is now no longer growing independent of other world economies. This aside, the example of South Korea gives significant pause to the claims made by the dependency theorists that international terms of trade militate against the economic development of countries in the Third World. The cost of this development in terms of human repression and misery is, however, altogether another story.

To summarise briefly: modernisation theorists, with their assumption that a free market economy and rapid industrialisation will bring about development, are in direct contradiction to the dependency theorists' claim that the world economy determines the nature of the relations – political and economic – between nations. One body of theory concentrates on internal issues; the other external issues. There is little surprise, therefore, that the two paradigms are seemingly impossible to reconcile, yet current thought amongst analysts is attempting to use elements of both perspectives to produce a new paradigm.

In 1984, Cumings proposed the bureaucratic authoritarian industrialising regime theory which attempted to show that such regimes, by virtue of their freedom from internal constraints or opposition, are able to put into practice severe policies which produce highly effective results (see B. Cumings, 'The Origin and Development of the Northeast Asian Political Economy: Industrial Sectors and Political Consequences', *International Organization* 38, 1–40). The role of the regime of the authoritarian state is a theme taken up by S. Haggard ('The Newly Industrializing Countries in the International System', in *World Politics* 38, 343–70), who, in effect, inverts elements of the central themes of both the modernisation and dependency theoretical perspectives. The developmentalist view of the free market as an agent in development is denied. Instead, it is held that a planned economy is a significant feature in ensuring developmental progress. Similarly, the notion that global economic systems dictate the nature of development within individual societies is replaced by the view that internal developments in specific countries largely determine the nature of international economic relations. To examine this newly emerging analytical perspective – which may be termed 'statist theory' – we shall examine briefly the economic and political record of Taiwan (previously Formosa), since that country appears to bear all the hallmarks of a bureaucratic authoritarian industrialising regime and has been singularly successful in development – at least in economic terms.

CASE STUDY: STATIST THEORY: AN EMERGING PARADIGM – TAIWAN

The beautiful island of Taiwan is situated off the coast of southeastern China and currently enjoys the reputation of being the most densely populated country of the entire world. The 13 890 square miles which constitute the land surface of the island has to provide accommodation for 19 600 000 people (mid-1987 figures; by the year 2000 the population is expected to be above 22 million).

Until the end of the nineteenth century Taiwan was under the control of China and had a mainly traditional agricultural economy which had changed little for many centuries. In large part this was due to the fact that the island was almost as remote from the political consciousness of the Chinese emperors as it was geographically inaccessible. The war between China and Japan which ended in 1895, though mainly concerned with the territorial rights over Korea, also affected Taiwan. Upon the closing of hostilities, the island was given up to Japanese control and the Japanese retained their dominion over it for fifty years until, in 1945, with the ending of the Second World War, Japan gave up all territorial claims. During the time of Japanese control the mainly subsistence agricultural base of the society was changed to become effectively an agricultural industry providing exports to Japan. It is apparent that the Japanese saw in Taiwan the ideal opportunity to acquire an offshore garden capable of providing abundant and cheap produce. In order to ensure this they made great improvements in agricultural methods and, through investment together with new techniques, brought about a significant increase in production. Also, for purposes of rationalisation, the Japanese introduced into the island economy a small number of industries which were closely connected with agricultural production, such as factories for the production of inorganic fertilisers and others to process and pack agricultural produce for shipment out as exports.

The ending of the Second World War saw Taiwan returned to Chinese control, and there followed a period of intense brutality and repression under the administration of Ch'en Yi, who was publicly executed following a national revolt in 1947. In 1948 the Kuomintang (Chinese Nationalist Party) forces were defeated in the Chinese Civil War of 1945–48, and their leaders were forced to take refuge in Taiwan. In 1949 the Kuomintang regime took effective control, with American backing, under the leadership of Chiang Kai-shek.

The period of the Korean War was very significant for the future of Taiwan since it came under the protection of the United States as part of that country's concern with maintaining a bulwark against the spread of communism throughout the world. The Chinese Nationalist government embarked upon a programme of economic development, and has been consistent in its powerful and stringent controls over the economy and the targets which were to be reached. In order to accommodate this massive increase in output and technological change, the government introduced a vocationally oriented education system, together with a martial law system which placed severe restrictions upon the rights of citizens.

The role of the state has been therefore apparently to ensure that a docile, utilitarian workforce became available so that policies of economic expansion could be carried through effectively, regardless of the human cost.

A number of theorists have pointed out that Taiwan is a model of free market capitalism which provides ample proof of the truth beneath the modernisationist theories (See G. Gilder, *Wealth and Poverty*, Basic Books, 1981; also, M. Levy, 'Modernization Exhumed', *Journal of Developing Societies* 2, 1–11). In addition, there are others who have pointed to the dependency induced in Taiwan by successive colonising and neo-colonialist powers, though they are virtually unanimous in the degree to which they emphasise the role of Taiwan's powerful regime in maintaining a strong sense of autonomy when confronted with overseas 'aid' packages (see T. Hayter, *Aid as Imperialism*, Penguin, 1971; also, (A. H. Amsden, 'The State and Taiwan's Economic Development', in *Bringing the State Back In*, P. B. Evans, D. Rueschemeyer, and T. Skocpol, (eds) CUP, 1985).

The 'Taiwan phenomenon' clearly shows up the inadequacies of both developmentalist and dependency theoretical schemes as explanatory models of contemporary events. It is insufficient to point out changes in the internal structure and characteristics, since, technology apart, many of the traditional institutions have apparently remained intact. Further, the traditional institutions and values seem to be highly compatible with the concept of a powerful, authoritarian regime. Equally, a major element in dependency theory – the notion that an indigenous elite in the pay of an external economic force will enforce external controls (compradorisation) – fails to match with the observed reality of Taiwanese economic affairs. In statist theory aspects of both previous theoretical strands are joined in order to produce a new explanatory paradigm. It is doubtful whether this paradigm can be applied universally because of quite specific cultural reasons, such as traditional acceptance of paternalism, subservience and passivity in the oriental culture generally and in Taiwan in particular, which produce a unique situation. Unless statist theory is significantly modified it may well be found wanting in attempts to apply it to Western cultural values.

PART 4

An overview

9 Aspects of development

Purely economic factors, such as lack of investment capital, are not the only characteristics upon which the functionalist/ modernisation theorists have based their analyses and against which radical theorists have argued fiercely. Frequently other 'explanations' are used in order to account for the existence, and continuation, of poverty in the Third World. We will now consider some of the other principal features frequently entering the debate on development, and briefly outline the main points of each issue.

Population and development

The specialised study of population statistics is known as 'demography' and is of importance to governments in order that they may try and predict future trends in population growth, composition and distribution. Information such as this helps in the formulation of social policy by providing data on probable demand for services such as housing, education and health-care provision. Demographers use rather complex statistical processes in order to make many of their predictions, but, essentially, information on changes in population can be derived from the measurement of just three variables: the birth-rate, the death-rate and migration (either between countries or internally in one country).

1 *The birth-rate* – usually defined as the number of live births per thousand of population in any given year. Sometimes it is referred

to as the 'fertility rate', which is defined as the number of live births per thousand women of child-bearing age (16–45 years) in any given year.

2 *The death-rate* (sometimes called the 'mortality rate' – defined as the number of deaths from all causes per thousand of population in any given year. One specific death-rate, the infant mortality rate (IMR) (which is the number of children born alive who die on, or before, their first birthday expressed per thousand of population in any given year) gives a good indication of the overall social conditions prevailing in any specific society.

3 *Migration* – defined as the movement in (*immi*gration) or, out (*emi*gration) of a country. It also refers to internal movement of population and is of interest in the analysis of the growth of towns and cities – a process known as 'urbanisation' (see p. 87).

Growth of population

Consider the following table of population figures for the United Kingdom:

1871	27 431 000	There has been a fluctuating, but steady growth
1881	31 014 000	in the size of population in the United Kingdom.
1891	34 264 000	This is because the birth-rate has
1901	38 236 000	consistently been greater than the death-rate.
1911	42 081 000	However, at the same time, the birth-rate has
1921	44 027 000	actually fallen though there has been an even
1931	46 038 000	more rapid decline in the death-rate. (Another
1951	50 225 000	way of expressing this last point is to look at
1961	52 708 000	the 'expectation of life', i.e., the length of
1971	55 200 000	time a person may expect to live from the time
1981	55 697 000	of birth.)

Source: *Facts in Focus*, HMSO, 1982

It is possible, from the analysis of demographic data, to see four main stages through which the growth of all populations pass. The first stage is when there is both a high birth-rate and a high death-rate; population increases very slowly during this stage. The second stage is typified by a continued high birth-rate but accompanied by a rapidly falling death-rate; here, population growth is very rapid indeed. In stage three there is a fall in both

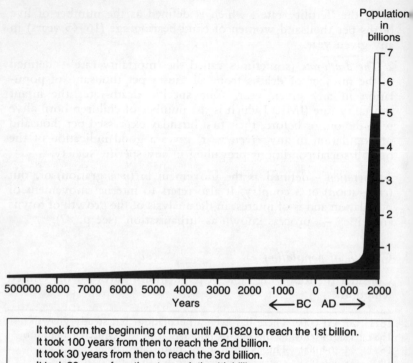

It took from the beginning of man until AD1820 to reach the 1st billion.
It took 100 years from then to reach the 2nd billion.
It took 30 years from then to reach the 3rd billion.
It took 20 years from then to reach the 4th billion.
It took 15 years from then to reach the 5th billion.

Source: Diagram adapted from C. Warn and P. Wilby, *Population and Development*, Macmillan Educational, 1986, p. 24

Figure 9.1   World population growth

the birth-rate and the death-rate (though the death-rate is still lower than the birth-rate); population growth still occurs although the rate of increase is slowing down. The final stage, typically, has a low birth-rate and a low-death rate; the population increases only very slowly, or may even decline slightly.

The population of the earth, taken as a whole, has followed the first two stages of the above model. In 1976 the number of human beings exceeded 4 billion (4 thousand million), since when the number has grown by more than 175 000 people every *day* (64

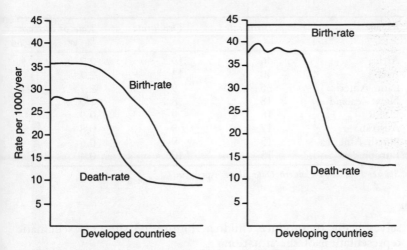

Figure 9.2   Differential population growth (schematic)

million every year), and the total figure reached 5 billion in 1987. Estimates based upon a continuation of the current growth rate of 1.7 per cent per annum show that early in the next century the population of the earth will reach 8 billion, and by the year 2100 it will be 12 billion (see Figure 9.1) (source: Population Reference Bureau, Washington, DC). Further analysis of population changes in different parts of the world, however, shows that some (mainly in the developed world) have gone through stages three and four, while others (mainly in the underdeveloped Third World) have remained at stage two. The figures for the Third World are quite staggering; for example, Egypt had a population of just 2 million in 1800 which, by 1978, had increased to 38 million. The Indian sub-continent has, in the last fifty years, doubled its population to an enormous 650 million human beings. Some indication of why this situation prevails can be seen schematically in Figure 9.2, where the birth-rates and death-rates of some developed countries are compared with those of some in the Third World, and in the table on page 78.

It must also be noted that most Third World countries tend to have a majority of their population under the age of 25 years. Such a situation has great significance for the potential dramatic increase in population size it signals as these young people them-

Region	Birth-rate	Death-rate	Rate of increase %/yr
Africa	46	19	2.7
Asia	40	13	2.7
Latin America	36	9	2.7
New Zealand	18	8	1.0
USSR	18	9	0.9
Australia	17	8	0.8
North America	15	9	0.6
Europe	15	10	0.4

Source: *Population Concern Data Sheet*, April 1987

selves begin to produce children. Figure 9.3 shows a schematic representation of the situation.

In keeping with other issues in social analysis, demography is a further area of contention, with commentators forming into two groups, roughly aligning with the 'positivists' on one side, and the 'Marxists' on the other. Those adopting the first position are, perhaps, typified by Paul Ehrlich, a biologist whose work *The Population Bomb* (Ballantyne, 1968) became one of the 'cult' books of the late 1960s and early 1970s. He has described how he first became aware of the population problem during one 'stinking hot night in Delhi':

> As we crawled through the city (by taxi), we entered a crowded slum area. The temperature was well over 100, and the air was a haze of dust and smoke. The streets seemed alive with people. People eating, people washing, people sleeping. People visiting, arguing and screaming. People thrusting their hands through the taxi window, begging. People defecating and urinating. People clinging to buses. People herding animals. People, people, people, people. As we moved slowly through the mob, hand horn squawking, the dust, noise, heat and the cooking fires gave the scene a hellish aspect.

For Ehrlich, then, it is the sheer size of population which is responsible for all the poverty, starvation, civil unrest, wars and environmental pollution around the world. Following the positivist scientific method of accurate measurement, the figures for

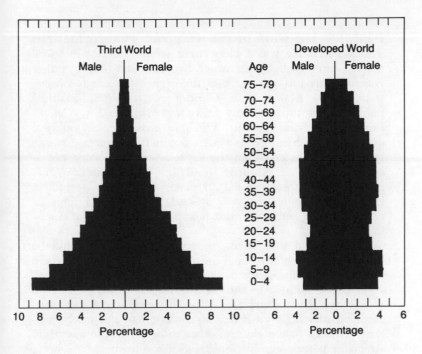

Figure 9.3   Population: composition by age

birth-rates and death-rates are found and compared with the rate of food production, malnutrition levels, and so on in specific societies. Conclusions are then drawn from these figures which, it is maintained, show clear causal connections between population size/growth and social problems.

In a later work Ehrlich, this time writing with his wife Anne, develops this theme by stating the Neo-Malthusian (Figure 9.4) view that the world is over-populated because the increase in population is outstripping the world's reserves of natural resources, and the capacity of the earth to produce sufficient quantities of food. In this they are quite specific, and maintain that 'The limits of human capability to produce food by conventional means have very nearly been reached' (*Population, Resources, Environment*, A. Ehrlich and P. R. Ehrlich, W. H. Freeman, 1970, pp. 146–7).

Figure 9.4 **The work of the Reverend Thomas Malthus**
Thomas Malthus was a clergyman whose interest in social
matters most probably stemmed from the fact that his father
was influenced by the work of the French thinker and social
analyst, the Marquis de Condorcet. In 1798, Malthus
published his most widely known work, the *Essay on the
Principles of Population*, in which he sets out his political
doctrines. His main thesis is that populations increase in size
at a much faster rate than the capacity of those same populations to provide essential foodstuffs. As a result, over a
period of time, many must starve or at the least be subject
to severe malnutrition, which leads to increased rates of
disease, unless some restraint is applied to the rate of population increase.

Malthus held that 'vice, misery and poverty' would be
instrumental in controlling the excesses of population, and
this meant, by implication, that any action to interfere with
what was thought of as the form of society ordained by God
was immoral and therefore sinful. Accordingly, it was seen
as unchristian to give help or protection to the sick, igno-
rant, maimed or the elderly, since to do so would adversely
affect the natural equilibrium of God's universe.

The alternative view to that of Ehrlich and Ehrlich is typified
by Avery M. Guest, assistant professor of sociology, Dartmouth
College, New Hampshire, USA, who, in a critique written for
Concerned Demography in 1970, concluded that:

the Ehrlich-type arguments have a great deal of appeal for the
US government. They place the burden of poverty in most of
the world on the high growth rates of the underdeveloped
countries rather than the present and historical actions of
Western society. Thus, we have little moral responsibility to
help these countries. Ehrlich's arguments place the cause of
poverty in the United States on the alleged inability of the poor
to control their family size. Thus the government does not
have to make serious efforts to change the system of wages so
the poor have decent incomes. The Ehrlich arguments also

provide an escape valve for the government in the area of pollution. Since Ehrlich sees people, not businesses, polluting, the government does not have to feel obligated to require pollution control by businesses.

One solution to what is seen as the 'Third World population problem' often advocated in the developed nations is a comprehensive family planning policy. This policy has its foundation in the positivist analysis of population which has been carried out by Western demographers. Whereas superficially their conclusions may appear to lead to wise counsel, upon some reflection they may be seen to be based upon only a partial analysis of the many factors involved.

Using the positivist approach, analysts in the developed nations measure the birth-rate in the Third World and relate this to the overall growth in population. Clearly, the decline in the death-rate is brought about by marginally improved living conditions, and this, together with the continued high birth-rate, causes population size to increase rapidly. From a purely analytical perspective the problem appears to have but one solution: to change the pattern of fertility through effective contraceptive measures developed in the affluent nations. However, as one commentator has stated: 'this is to fall into what has been well termed the technological fallacy which has long marked Western thinking . . . a kind of blind faith in the gadgetry of contraception' (*The Population Explosion: an Interdisciplinary Approach*, Open University, Unit D100, 1972).

An alternative view has suggested that it is important to take note of the wider social aspects of human patterns of fertility by including factors such as religious belief, marriage customs, educational level, and the persistence of traditional values such as the degree of masculinity being gauged by the number of children produced. In addition, it is important to take into account the meaning of having children in different cultures: to work as sources of income; to look after one in one's old age; to act as a source of status, and so on. Mahmood Mamdani, in *The Myth of Population Control*, has shown that a birth-control programme attempted in India failed because there was insufficient understanding of such factors by the Indian government and the Ford Foundation which were sponsoring the experimental programme. Mamdani has claimed that

If we are to come to a true understanding of the 'population problem' – one that comes to terms not only with the theoretical optimism of the 'overpopulation' theorists, but also with the rather pessimistic results of the birth control programs – we need a different method. Central to this new method must be an understanding that the motivations of men and women originate in their social experience. Motivations do not exist in the abstract; their roots are to be found in a given social structure.

　　(M. Mamdani, *The Myth of Population Control*, Monthly Review Press, 1972, p. 20)

Other writers have also maintained that to concentrate upon the increase in population in Third World nations is to miss a vital point – which is that, in the developed industrial nations, the majority of the population follow a style of life which is extremely wasteful of the scarce resources of this planet. Overwhelmingly, the industrial nations use most of the available raw materials and energy produced on earth, yet this is done seemingly with scant regard for their finite nature. In Figure 9.6 (E. McGraw, 'Sharing the Earth's Resources', in *Population Today*, Kaye & Ward, 1979, p. 90) may be seen the raw materials involved in the production of one motor car. This of course does not include the oil reserves used to lubricate and to propel it – usually to transport just one person in the massive queues of traffic which are to be seen each day in the major cities of the industrial nations. Figure 9.5 shows graphically the differential use of energy between the developed, industrial nations and the underdeveloped world.

Food production would appear to be a relatively small problem, for, in the prosperous industrial nations, there are massive surpluses stockpiled throughout Europe and the USA, and superficially the question appears one of rationalising the distribution system. However, on a global scale, the production of food is a significant problem which requires an urgent solution to be found. One possible way out of what has been termed the 'protein famine' may be to change the eating habits of the consumers. The production of protein from animal flesh is a highly inefficient method because the productive cycle involves many separate stages, all of which use significant amounts of expensive energy:

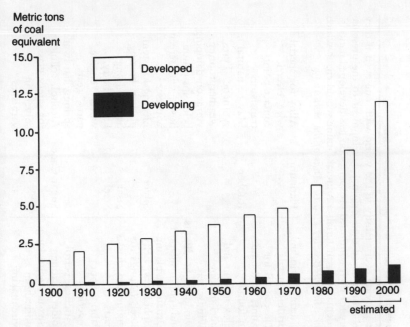

Metric tons of coal equivalent

Developed

Developing

1900 1910 1920 1930 1940 1950 1960 1970 1980 1990 2000
estimated

Source: United Nations in B. Ward and R. Dubos, *Only One Earth*, Penguin, 1976, p. 241

Figure 9.5 Developed and developing countries' energy consumption per capita

Grain – (*transport*) – Animal – (*transport*) – Slaughter – (*transport*) – Processing – (*transport; canning; refrigeration, etc.*) – Preparation – (*cooking*) – Consumption.

More importantly, perhaps, is another feature of meat production which is significant: the amount of available protein produced per acre from grazing livestock is much lower than if the same area of land was sown with vegetable protein crops. Of course, some improvement can be made by using 'factory farming' methods and introducing hormones and so on into animal feed to induce faster growth, but, leaving aside moral and health questions, from an efficiency standpoint these methods, too, are inherently wasteful of resources.

Figure 9.6   The 59 materials used in the production of one motor vehicle

A family car. But the earth's limited resources cannot provide every family in the world with one even if they could afford it. 'Paradoxically, the industrial countries which owed their original development to the presence of mineral resources, particularly iron and coal, now rely for their continued prosperity on less developed nations. If the less developed nations were to develop a similar demand for materials a mineral famine would ensue which would have repercussions throughout the world.' (*The Mitchell Beazley Concise Atlas of the Earth*)

Material	Use	Material	Use	Material	Use
Aluminium	Engine parts, transmission parts, spark plugs, castings, trim mouldings	Diamonds	Cutting, grinding, drilling metals	Platinum	Alloy for special wire, electric contact points, transistors
Asbestos	Brake linings, gaskets, sound deadeners	Flaxseed	Linseed oil for paint, sand binder in foundry	Rubber	May be natural or synthetic. Tyres, weatherproofing, vibration damping, belts, insulation, hoses, windscreen wipers
Barite	Fillers for paints, rubber, plastics	Fluorspar	Flux in iron and steel making		
Bauxite	Ore for metal aluminium	Glass	Windscreen, windows, headlights and spun insulation	Silver	Electrical system, plating, brazing
Beeswax	Wire insulation, adhesives	Gold	Ornament plating	Sisal	Seat padding
Bismuth	Hardens lead, tin, steel	Hides	Upholstery, belts	Steel	Frame body, wheels, engine parts, gears, springs, hardware
Borax	For smelting and special steels	Iron Ore	Steel, castings for engine and chassis parts		
		Jute	Fabric, floor coverings	Sugar Cane	Alcohol, cellulose for safety glass, solvent in varnishes
Cadmium	Alloy to harden copper, electropainting, paints	Lead	Batteries, petrol, solder, plating		
		Lime	Flux in steelmaking, lubricant in wire making		

Item	Uses	Item	Uses	Item	Uses
Carbon	Rubber making, paints, electrodes, graphite seals, electrical brushes	Magnesite	Mineral ore if magnesium	Sulphur	Vulcanising rubber, lubricant, additives, steel
Cattle	Glue, glycerines, hides, hair for air cleaners	Magnesium	Light alloys for engine parts	Textiles	Upholstery, lining, tyres
		Manganese	Steel making	Tin	Plating, alloys, solder
Chemicals	Nylon, synthetic rubber, plastics	Mercury	Mirrors, amalgams with other metals, switches	Tungsten	Special steel, lamp filaments
Chromite	Ore produces chromium used for plating, alloys	Mica	Electrical insulators	Turpentine	Paints
Clay	Rubber filler, modelling	Mohair	Upholstery, carpets	Vanadium	Special steel
		Molybdenum	Steel alloys, fine wire, grease, paint	Wheat Straw	Strawboards, panels
Coal	Iron and steel making, nylon, solvents, tars fuel	Nickel	Alloyed with steel, copper, other metals, plating	Wood	Cellulose for safety glass, packing cases, paper, fibre board, truck body parts
Cobalt	Steel making	Paint	Body and interior finish		
Coconut Oil	Paints, lacquers	Paper	Insulation, gaskets, soundproofing, filters	Wool	Upholstery, carpeting, felt
Columbium	Stainless steel			Zinc	Batteries, alloy for die-cast parts, plating
Copper	Electrical system, radiator, plated parts, alloys	Petroleum	Petrol, oil, lubricants, synthetics, solvents		
Cork	Gaskets, insulation	Plastics	Body and engine parts, trim, upholstery	Zirconium	Alloy in steel and copper making, aluminium castings
Cotton	Wadding, padding, felt tyres, insulation, thread				

from: E. McGraw, *Population Today*, Kaye & Ward, 1979, p. 90.

A further dimension is the fact that Third World nations are inhibited from developing their own agricultural economic sector by a combination of factors, both natural and political in origin. First, there is the question of adverse climatic and soil conditions which exist in many of these areas. Also it has been estimated that millions of acres of land suitable for cultivation go to waste each year due to the demands of road-building, industrialisation, deforestation (for newsprint and so on) and from soil erosion. A British government publication in 1975 indicated that over 40 000 acres of agricultural land in Britain every year were being given over to house-building, industrial expansion and the demands of leisure pursuits. Although at the moment these are formidable obstacles, particularly keenly felt in the Third World, they are not insurmountable given the determination to succeed with projects such as irrigation and soil improvement. As an International Planned Parenthood Federation booklet points out: 'methods of prevention are known. . . . Careful maintenance of tree and plant cover of the soil, minimum tillage, multi-layer cropping, terracing and so on are essential. More efficient use of energy, and transition to renewable energy sources, including fuelwood plantations, will also be needed' (P. Harrison and J. Rowley, 'Human Numbers, Human Needs', IPPF, 1984, p. 38).

Second, there is another aspect of this same matter, which is the unwillingness of sectarian interests within the developed nations to see the Third World begin to produce foodstuffs on a large scale. Curious as this may seem it is, in reality, based upon sound capitalist economic principles of supply and demand. World commodity prices are based upon prevailing supply, and any glut in the market will have a harmful effect upon prices, and hence the profitability, of the agricultural 'industry' of the developed nations. More sinister perhaps is the wider political implication of such policies exemplified by the pronouncements of people such as Lyle P. Schertz, of the US Department of Foreign Affairs:

> With strong demand, negligible stocks, and high prices it is not now advantageous to US agriculture to move significant amounts of food under PL480 (Food for Peace). . . . Neither we nor other rich countries are willing to forego substantial foreign exchange earnings in the interest of feeding the poor.

Or that of Dan Ellerman (US National Security Council):

To give food aid to countries just because people are starving is a pretty weak reason.

Or of the US Central Intelligence Agency, Office of Political Research:

In a cooler and therefore hungrier world, the US near monopoly as a food exporter . . . could give the US a measure of power it never had before – possibly an economic and political dominance greater than that of the immediate post-World War II years. . . . Washington would acquire vital life and death power over the fate of multitudes of the needy.
(Quoted in A. G. Frank, *Crisis: In the Third World*, Heinemann Educational, 1981, p. 63).

Urbanisation

The change from an agrarian to an industrial mode of production which occurred in Britain with the Industrial Revolution led to the movement of population away from the countryside to form the great towns and cities of today. This process is known as 'urbanisation', and can be defined as the rate of increase in the proportion of a given population living in towns or cities.

The causes of urbanisation are many and often complex. In the early stages of the Industrial Revolution many people became displaced from their roots in agriculture and moved in search of work and, perhaps, the hope of an improved quality of life for themselves and their children. In later stages of industrial development much of the administrative and economic control is centred in the larger, or capital cities. The slowing down of the rate at which population is growing in the developed nations has effectively slowed down the process of urbanisation. Indeed, there is some evidence that a reversal of the process is beginning in some of the larger cities of Europe, as, for example, recent figures for London indicate.

Throughout the Third World, however, as B. Roberts has pointed out (*Cities and Peasants*, Edward Arnold, 1978), there is a massive proliferation of urbanisation which is taking place throughout the underdeveloped southern hemisphere. The significant difference between the current Third World process and that which occurred, historically, in the industrial areas of the developed world is that it is happening without any significant growth of industry. What results is the massive sprawl of 'shanty towns' which the poor construct from the cast-off waste of their more affluent fellow citizens. There are millions of human beings living in these conditions throughout the Third World (and, increasingly, though on a very much reduced scale, in the affluent Western nations). Individuals and their families are drawn to the large centres of population because there they are more likely to find an income (through begging), food and clothing (through foraging and cast-offs).

Many cities in the Third World are now truly astronomic in their size of population; for example, Mexico City, perhaps the largest urban mass in the developing world, has over 17 million inhabitants (1980 estimate) and is thought set to reach more than 30 million inhabitants by the turn of the twenty-first century. The table opposite shows the fastest growing cities, all of which are in the Third World.

The Report of the United Nations Conference on Human Settlements, *Habitat*, published in 1976, indicated that, in order adequately to house every family on Earth in need of a home, over one billion new dwellings would have to be constructed. The policies aimed at developing the Third World which are motivated by the modernisation theorists' approach have, in the opinion of many observers, been positively harmful instead of beneficial to the population. Hoogvelt, for example, has argued that 'crash programmes both of industrialisation and of agricultural modernisation set adrift a rural proletariat which flocked to towns causing over-urbanisation rather than urbanisation' (A. M. M. Hoogvelt, *The Sociology of Developing Societies*, 2nd edn, 1983, Macmillan, p. 61).

The results of continued deprivation and squalor in an urban environment and an example of some of the consequences which result from Third World urbanisation have been graphically set out by Robin Cohen in his description of African conditions:

> Many Africans migrating to the cities found themselves without jobs, or unable to get those they aspired to. Some accommodated themselves to a socially disapproved existence as pimps, touts, prostitutes, or thieves, living often at the margins of subsistence or preying, like parasites, on what few pickings a capital city of an impoverished country can offer. Others swelled the ranks of those who staff the industries,

Cities with one million or more people

Largest cities	Population (millions) 1985	Growth rate (%)
1 Tokyo	25.2	69
2 New York	18.8	15
3 Shanghai	14.3	43
4 Los Angeles	13.7	63
5 Calcutta	12.1	75
6 Peking	12.0	71
7 Osaka	11.8	55
8 Buenos Aires	11.7	39
9 Rio de Janeiro	11.4	68
10 London	11.1	6
11 Paris	10.9	30
12 Moscow	8.0	13

Fastest-growing cities	Population (millions) 1985	Growth rate (%)
1 Mexico City	17.9	113
2 Sao Paulo	16.8	115
3 Bombay	12.1	109
4 Seoul	10.3	124
5 Karachi	9.2	163
6 Tehran	7.9	132
7 Bangkok	7.1	137
8 Bogota	6.4	146
9 Lima	6.2	121
10 Baghdad	4.9	145
11 Lagos	4.0	186
12 Bandung	4.1	242

Source: Adapted from E. McGraw, *Population Today*, Kaye & Ward, p. 58

small trades and services that blanket the landscape of any African city. This sector of the urban economy, described often nowadays as the 'informal sector', in fact accounts for a considerable degree of urban employment. . . . A space on the workshop floor is living accommodation, and pocket money barely covers the means of survival, while the El Dorado to the apprentice, namely a workshop of his own, is difficult to finance and may indeed never materialise.

(Robin Cohen, 'The Emergence of Wage Labor', in C. Allen and G. Williams (eds), *Sociology of Developing Societies: Sub-Saharan Africa*, Macmillan, 1982, p. 39)

Education and development

Education is an essential aspect of human life, both for individuals and for entire nations. If the accumulated knowledge, skills and traditional cultural values are not transmitted from one generation to the next, then the society cannot progress and will remain intellectually and culturally stagnant. Informal education ensures that the young of a society acquire the patterns of behaviour through socialisation which will enable them to find an acceptance with their peers. Formal education, on the other hand, is vital for the production of people with increasingly specialised skills which are required as the demands of new, changing technology increase.

Third World nations, not surprisingly, have low levels of attainment in formal education. According to United Nations statistics there were, in 1980, thirty-four nations in which over 80 per cent of the population were illiterate. The same source also states that approximately 50 per cent of all adults in the developing nations of the Third World were illiterate as recently as 1975.

The explanations for this situation are, of course, many and varied. One theory asserts that poor families in underdeveloped regions are faced with the dilemma of having to choose to keep their young in work as valuable, much needed, sources of income; or to let them be a 'burden upon the hearth' and be permitted to have some education in the hope of longer-term improvement in life chances. Recent figures from the International Labour Organisation, a body analysing all aspects of child labour in the Third World, seem to confirm the impression that most Third World families yield to economic pressures and send their children out to work long hours, for low pay, in appalling conditions. In short, it may be said that such a situation is similar to that which was prevalent in any European nation during the early stages of industrialisation.

The amount of illiteracy prevalent in the underdeveloped nations is yet another characteristic used by modernisation theorists to explain the continued lack of economic growth. The lack of skills which are relevant to new and advancing technology is seen to result from a lack of adequate educational and training provision. Yet the aid agencies of the developed nations are proud of their record in the field of education; for example, the Overseas

Development Administration of Great Britain has made the claim that

> At present we help finance more than 160 British advisers in 50 countries working on our aid projects. About 150 others are working in government educational institutions, with their salaries made up to British levels through the aid programme. Among the many foreign students studying in Britain are some 12 000 from developing countries funded from our aid programme.
> Britain spent £104 million on education and training world-wide in 1985.

There would appear to be a conflicting issue here; on the one hand, analysts are maintaining that the lack of trained personnel is holding back progress in the Third World; on the other, aid agencies maintain they have spent, and continue to spend large sums on education and training. As Walter Rodney has pointed out:

> It is difficult to see how they can have it both ways. If independent Africa is still without the benefits of modern education (as it is) then 75 years of colonial exploitation undoubtedly have something to do with that state of affairs; and the absurdity is so much greater when one contemplates how much Africa produced in that period and how much of that went to develop all aspects of European capitalist society, including their educational institutions. Cecil Rhodes could afford to leave a legacy of lavish scholarships to white students for study at Oxford University, having made a fortune from exploiting Africa and Africans.
> (W. Rodney, *How Europe Underdeveloped Africa*, Bogle L'Ouverture Publications, 1972, p. 270)

Taking the Third World nations as a whole, it is fair to say that the major advances which have been made in science and in technology have not, as yet, percolated into their educational programmes. There is, of course, much new technology available in parts of the Third World – computers in banks, and so on – but very few native people possess the knowledge to use it. Equally, this is not to imply that there is no advanced education in the Third World – far from it; the problem appears to be that to train relatively few people in the sophisticated skills of, for example, engineering, science and medicine does little or nothing for the welfare of the vast majority for whom such technology is meaningless. It can scarcely be of importance for the Indian peasant to know that his country possesses advanced computer technology when his own knowledge precludes successful irrigation of his crops.

Typically, then, highly trained Third World personnel will leave their native land lured by the possibility of earning a much higher income and finding an improved quality of life in the developed economies. As the World Health Organisation has repeatedly indicated, for example, India alone has lost many millions of pounds through educating doctors who, upon qualifying, take their skills overseas to nations already infinitely better endowed with medical care facilities. (In 1975, the number of doctors for every 10 000 people in the Third World was 28; in the same year, the figure for the developed nations was 190 per 10 000 people.) There are many of the more wealthy elite who can afford the advantage of an education for their children in the countries of the developed world. This has a dual effect, First, it ensures that the previous traditional values of the 'old country' are even further submerged and subordinated to the values of advanced industrial society. Second, the process makes sure that there is a self-recruitment of elites in the developing country and that, effectively, a dynastic effect emerges with a consolidated elite group retaining wealth, privilege and power.

Education is not only concerned with the transmission of skills however; it is also concerned with passing on social and personal skills, and with shaping overall attitudes to life. Thus, through the medium of mass educational communication, people find their lives controlled in subtle, but very firm, ways. This process is, of course, the domain of the professional advertising people and the psychologists. Through slick advertising, multinational companies are able to create demand for their products within the nations of the Third World; products which frequently lack the protection of trading standards control that is so evident in the developed nations. Tobacco products, for example, have been subject to stringent scrutiny and legislation in the West as health risks are widely publicised. As the sales in the developed world have fallen, so the advertising investment in the Third World has correspondingly risen. Ivan Illich has called the process by which the multinationals increase their markets within the Third World

'Cocacolonisation'. The perceived needs of the people in the Third World for basic food, clothing and shelter become, by this process, translated into wants which relate clearly to the products more fitted to the consumer culture of the affluent nations. Illich has explained the process as 'the translation of thirst into the need for a Coke. This kind of reification occurs in the manipulation of primary human needs by vast bureaucratic organisations which have succeeded in dominating the imagination of potential customers' (I. Illich, 'Outwitting the Developed Countries', in *Underdevelopment and Development: the Third World Today*, H. Bernstein (ed.), Penguin, 1973).

Through advertising the peoples of the Third World are thus encouraged to buy many of the consumer goods put up for sale by the affluent nations (though frequently manufactured in other parts of the Third World!). This has a harmful effect upon the quality of life overall in two ways: first, the individual is living in an illusion of affluence with, say, a television set amongst the squalor of a shanty town; second, and far more serious, is the fact that individuals may sell wholesome food produced by themselves locally in order to purchase processed foodstuffs from the affluent nations.

For example, a person in the Third World may sell eggs in order to purchase artificial baby food in the belief that she is giving her baby a better start in life. The sales of baby food have been steadily falling as a result of 'breast is best' advice which follows the increased tendency for more natural forms of child-birth and childcare to be used throughout the developed world. Third World women, especially in Africa, have been subjected to much advertising of powdered milk for bottle feeding. The advertisers try to change the habits of the mothers away from breast feeding by creating an image of 'modernity' in relation to the 'scientifically prepared' baby food (David Morley, *Paediatric Priorities in the Developing World*, 1973, Butterworth). If this fundamentally safe product is mixed with water from a polluted source (as it frequently is in the developing world), then a serious potential risk to health is created.

Health and development

A comparison between health-care provision in the developed

nations and that in the Third World shows that, in keeping with expectations, the Third World lags far behind. This is, of course, scarcely surprising since the health enjoyed by an individual cannot be viewed in isolation from other social and economic indicators of quality of life. One good indication of the overall standard of health-care provision within a nation is the statistics for infant mortality rates (IMR); that is, the number of children per thousand of population who die on, or before, their first birthday. Consider the following table:

Region	IMR (per 1000/yr)
World average	99
Africa	147
Asia	105
South America	98
Latin America	84
Soviet Union	28
Europe	20
USA and Canada	15

Source: Population Reference Bureau Reference Sheet, April 1987

It is clear from the above that there is a definite causal connection between social and environmental conditions and the level of infant mortality. This is perhaps highlighted by a comparison between the IMR in different sectors of southern Africa. In the affluent white area, the IMR is only 14 per thousand per year, whereas in the black regions of Namibia and Swaziland the rates are 177 and 168 per thousand per year respectively.

Of those children in the Third World who survive past their first birthday, a further third will die before their fifth birthday, usually from diseases which are easily preventable (given access to medical resources), or from malnutrition, which is totally preventable (given access to food). Many of those who survive into teenage and adulthood are left permanently scarred by physical and/or mental retardation, and this has a 'knock-on' effect which passes through into future generations.

The adults in the Third World are also subject to a much higher incidence of infections which are easily preventable given adequate diet. In the areas of greatest poverty the main problems are malnourishment and starvation, conditions which lead to chronic weakness and a reduced interest in, or capacity for, any form of physical or mental effort. Female adults face significant extra problems by virtue of their biological role as mothers: many pregnancies, frequent childbirth or spontaneous abortion, together with prolonged periods of breast feeding, do much more to undermine the health of women in underdeveloped nations.

It became clear from many studies carried out in the developed nations of the industrial world that conditions of poverty and squalor led to a high level of disease and mortality. Conditions in the towns and cities of the early Industrial Revolution in Britain were very harsh, with little or no sanitation and a poor diet. Little was done about general levels of public health, however, until the late nineteenth century. Between about 1850 and the turn of the twentieth century many Public Health Acts were passed, which led to water and sewage being separated (that is, water was piped instead of being drawn from rivers or wells); and the general conditions were improved by better drainage, lighting and overall sanitation. Medical advances also improved the standard of care of women and children during childbirth and after. The overall level of infant mortality began to fall after 1902, when the Certification of Midwives Act ensured that only properly trained people could assist women in childbirth. By 1912, the level of infant mortality had fallen to 95 per thousand per year. Still, however, conditions in the industrialised nations could not be thought of as good. Indeed, many of the recruits into the British Army for the Boer War (1899–1902) were in such a poor physical condition that a 'Committee on Physical Deterioration' advised the government of the day of the need to provide school meals and regular medical inspection of children.

The vast majority of people in the Third World live in social conditions which are equal to, if not significantly worse than, those described in the work of the early reformers in Britain. This is in spite of the fact that most of the Third World has, for a considerable time, been subject to colonising powers from Europe. The majority of the Third World is still agricultural, and there remains evidence of the influence retained by the colonial or ex-colonial powers through multinational companies. A substantial proportion of Third World land remains taken up with the production of food and other extractive raw materials for shipment out to the developed world. This has great significance for the native diet and level of nutrition, which inevitably declines. In addition, there are many examples of workers being forced to work long hours in dangerous and unhealthy conditions which also contribute to the general level of debility and sickness – as, for example, in the mines of South Africa and the sugar plantations of the Caribbean.

Even if all the food grown was actually consumed by the native population they would still face the added problem of being unable satisfactorily to digest what food they managed to eat. A recent survey carried out by the Pan-American Health Organisation looked at the countries of Latin America, and found that between 70 and 90 per cent of all infant deaths occurred because of illnesses caused by faecal bacteria, airborne 'droplet' infection or malnutrition. The latter cause was isolated as the major contributor to almost 60 per cent of deaths, and, of course, because of the weakness following malnutrition, it may clearly be associated with most of the other infant deaths.

In the sociological analysis of health-care provision there are again the same major differences of approach to the same problems. The 'functionalist' argument, which is perhaps stated in its purest form by Parsons, views illness as resulting from a deliberate and conscious action by the patient. In his book *The Social System*, he stated:

> To take the simplest kind of case, differential exposure to injuries or to infection is certainly motivated, and the role of unconscious wishes to be injured or to fall ill in such cases has been clearly demonstrated. Then there is the whole range of 'psychosomatic' illness about which knowledge has been rapidly accumulating in recent years. Finally, there is the field of 'mental' disease, the symptoms of which occur mainly on a behavioural level.
> (The Free Press, 1951, pp. 430–1)

The opposing view, mainly from a Marxist standpoint, claims that ill health is caused by the systematic destruction of the Third World's natural resources in order to satisfy the requirements of capitalist social and economic conditions. During the period of colonial domination, as Doyal points out, traditional methods of health care, together with established patterns of social interaction with the environment were changed. These radical changes were instrumental in creating conditions which led to greater incidence of disease (L. Doyal, *The Political Economy of Health*, Pluto Press, 1979).

Further, it is argued that, with the development of the industrial system, and the requirements of a skilled workforce, medical care became an important component in ensuring that power differentials were retained, and thus that the interests of capitalism were maintained. This was possible because the break-up of the extended family meant that the workers were required to be cared for by the state. In consequence the medical profession became a sort of 'filter' through which sick people were to go in order to be approved as 'bona fide' and so deserving of state assistance. Since the medical profession was itself an integral part of the capitalist establishment, recruitment into the profession was restricted to those whose social background indicated their 'reliability'. This restricted entry meant, in addition, that trained medical personnel had a scarcity value rendering them eligible for the income and status commensurate with such a condition.

The number of trained personnel involved in health care within the Third World has risen steadily but it has not kept pace with the rise in population. In the developed world, the number of doctors per 100 000 population rose from 143 in 1965 to 190 ten years later. During the same period in the Third World, the figure rose from 24 to 28 doctors per 100 000 people (see Figure 9.7).

Some researchers have argued that the services which are provided in the Third World originate from the wrong philosophy and so do not even begin to meet the real needs of the people. It is all well and good, they argue, pushing forward the frontiers of medical science, but the really effective work is in the field of preventive medicine. Transplant surgery may well be superb technologically, but clean water, adequate diet and housing would prevent more illness and save more lives in one day than a whole year of sophisticated surgery.

Figure 9.7 **National coverage of health staff per 100 000 of population**

Developed nations		Developing nations
516	Midwives/nurses	53
190	Doctors	28
61	Dentists/technicians	7
53	Chemists (pharmacists)	9

Source: 1975 Figures from World Health Statistics, vol. 33, no. 2

Military, education and health expenditures compared

	Military % of GNP	Education % of GNP	Health % of GNP
Jordan	12.0	4.0	1.0
Iraq	9.0	3.0	0.6
Iran	13.5	3.0	1.4
Egypt	20.0	5.4	2.4
Israel	31.0	4.0	1.7
Pakistan	7.8	1.3	0.5
Malaysia	4.8	5.0	1.8
India	3.0	2.0	0.9
Indonesia	3.0	2.4	0.2
Cyprus	2.0	3.7	1.5
Turkey	3.7	2.8	0.7
Greece	4.0	1.8	1.0
Nigeria	3.7	3.16	0.2
Somalia	7.0	2.4	2.8
Tanzania	3.0	3.5	2.0
Zambia	3.0	5.0	2.0
Brazil	2.0	3.5	0.1
Chile	2.0	3.8	2.0
Peru	3.0	4.0	1.0
Colombia	0.9	2.0	0.9
United Kingdom	5.0	6.0	4.6
United States	6.0	5.6	2.7
Sweden	3.5	6.8	5.5
Netherlands	3.0	6.0	4.6
Australia	2.6	5.0	1.7
New Zealand	1.7	4.6	5.0
Bulgaria	2.9	4.0	2.0
USSR	11.9	5.9	2.0
Yugoslavia	4.7	4.7	0.7
Poland	2.9	4.0	3.0

Notes:

1 The national military expenditures used are current and capital expenditures to meet the needs of the armed forces. They include military assistance to foreign countries and the military components of nuclear, space and research and development programmes.
2 The public education expenditure used represent current and capital expenditures by governments for public education and subsidised private education for pre-school through university levels.
3 The public health expenditures used represent current and capital expenditures by governments for medical care and other health services.
Source: World Military and Social Expenditures. The Rockefeller Foundation 1977 by Mrs. Ruth Sivard; quoted in E. McGraw, *Population Today*, Kaye & Ward, 1979, p. 47

This brings the debate over health and health-care provision firmly into the realm of political debate for, clearly, most illness among people in the Third World is the result of poverty and lack of social development. The debate surrounding the causes of Third World poverty still rages on; is it lack of investment capital and so on, or the continued exploitation of the underdeveloped by the developed nations? Whatever the cause, the fact remains that there is such poverty – and it exists *now*.

The level of input into actually curing the mass of people can be seen to be severely limited; not least, this is caused by a shortage of trained personnel on the ground. Why are medically trained people so scarce? The answer is obvious: because so few of them are trained, and those that are receive a lengthy training covering all aspects of disease and curative measures. The training is both long and demanding, but, we must ask, is it effective?

Historically, doctors have been seen as the only people capable of dealing effectively with disease, yet, for most of their time in the field, they are called upon to deal with only the most mundane illnesses requiring little diagnostic skill and which could easily be prevented if resources were properly allocated. The World Health Organisation has estimated that the total cost of primary health care in the developing world using less trained, but hopefully equally effective, personnel would approximate to only about US$100 per head per year.

10 Statistics and documentary readings

The quantitative measurement of human society in order to describe social events and to support specific opinions and inferences about their nature is a fundamental feature of sociology. The authoritative status accorded to sociological data in the form of charts, tables and graphs and so on largely derives from the early 'scientific' origins of sociology. More specifically, statistics are central to one 'school' of sociology – the positivist – and have helped to formulate much of the ideological underpinning for the social and economic policies of Western governments.

Statistics are now widely available and are frequently presented in convenient (though occasionally misleading) forms. There is, however, a fundamental theoretical problem concerning the use of statistics as a means of sociological investigation. Basically, the difficulty concerns the way in which the statistics are gathered and, perhaps more importantly, how they are interpreted. In other words, positivist social analysts can measure social events as 'hard facts' in the manner of the natural scientists. This, however, in the view of critics, is to misinterpret social events or, more accurately, not to interpret them at all. A more valuable method of analysis in the view of anti-positivist sociologists might be to try and understand the meaning which individuals assign to their social actions and, through empathy, attempt to gain insight into the life experiences of others.

There is no easy solution to this schism in theoretical sociology. All is not lost, however, for most sociology uses statistical data at some time or other, even if they are only to provide a basis for debate over interpretation. In particular, since developmental sociology began with, and still employs, quantitative facts, statistical data are of particular relevance. The way in which this information is gathered and interpreted is, of course, open to the individual analyst's choice. (Readers may find a companion volume in the same series as this present work especially useful in understanding the different approaches: *Methods in Sociology* by Murray Morison.) What follows in this chapter is a small sample of the statistical data relating to development which, it is hoped, will prove to be a stimulus to further analysis and debate.

Background demographic data

In 1987 there were 37 countries having an annual percentage increase in population of 3.0 or more (see Figure 10.1, page 107). At this order of increase it is estimated that the populations of these countries will increase by a factor of between four or six within the next fifty years. Taking an overall figure for the world's population, the average rate of increase is slowing down – in 1987 it was 1.7 per cent – but the process is not uniform. A closer examination of the figures for the developed world compared with the less developed shows the following:

Region	Annual natural increase (%)
Developed world	0.5
Less developed world	2.1
Less developed world (excl. China)	2.4

Source: 1987 World Population Data Sheet

The rate of growth in the developed regions is expected to continue to fall at least into the first quarter of the next century. Thus, the developed northern hemisphere will see only a comparatively small increase in total population. It is in the impoverished southern hemisphere that the greatest increase in population will occur, with estimates of yearly total increase exceeding 80 million people.

Within the Third World as a whole, the area with the greatest annual percentage increase in population is the continent of Africa. This is due to a combination of factors, but mainly the sudden and dramatic fall in the death-rate over the past thirty years or so (from over 30 per thousand, to 16 per thousand per year), combined with birth-rates which have remained consistently high at an average of 44 live births per thousand per year.

It is not only population size and rate of population growth which indicate potential areas of demographic difficulty. Of equal, if not greater, significance is the number of people per square mile (or kilometre) within a nation. Density of population has a profound significance for social relationships. There is ample psychological evidence to show that high density increases stress, discord and unrest. In addition, the higher the density, the greater are the logistical problems of providing the basic requirements of adequate food, shelter and so on. The most densely populated European countries – Holland and Belgium – have population densities of just over 300 people per square kilometre. This must be compared with the figures for Third World countries such as Nigeria, Bangladesh and Rwanda, which currently support more than double this density of population. The expectations are that the figure for Bangladesh, for example, will increase from its 1980 figure of 675 people per square kilometre to reach a staggering 3000 people per square kilometre by the year 2100 (source: World Bank, *World Tables*, Washington, DC, 1980).

Another feature of this increase in population density needs to be taken into account. The population will not be evenly distributed over the whole surface area of the country. Indeed, some land is simply unsuitable for settlement due to its hostile climate and other factors. Equally, as more and more land becomes infertile through desertification and other results of human mismanagement, the people in these Third World areas will tend to migrate towards the larger centres of population in the search for an improved quality of life. This urbanisation process is, of course, very similar to that experienced historically within the developed countries. The process is identical in effect if not in origin. The scale of the internal migration of population towards urban centres is of massive proportions. For example, it is apparent that there has been a migration of people from rural to urban areas of Third World countries in the order of approximately 0.6 per cent per annum since 1960 (*World Population Trends and Policies 1981 Monitoring Report*). This appears to be such a small amount that, at first, it may seem almost innocuous. It is only when this is translated into actual numbers of human beings that the full impact of the situation may truly be felt: 0.6 per cent per annum amounts to approximately 20 million people moving into already crowded towns and cities every year.

READING 1 is taken from Gunder Frank's *Latin America: Underdevelopment or Revolution*, in which he takes issue with the interpretation of statistical evidence relating to the nature of capital flow between developed and underdeveloped nations.

READING 2 is taken from an Indian media article, and presents statistical evidence about population growth and the increasing proportion of people in the underdeveloped world who live in urban centres.

READING 3, from the International Planned Parenthood Federation, continues the theme of commenting upon the effects of a growing population by presenting data on food production and distribution under conditions of high rates of population increase and density.

READING 4 looks at another major problem created by rapid population increase: the question of finding employment for all the people. This is significantly more difficult when the levels of technology in the developed world have increased to the point where machines replace labour. As this technology is exported to the developing countries, the demand for labour will not be nearly high enough to provide jobs for all.

Reading 1   Who is supporting whom?

The conservative estimates of the United States Department of Commerce show that between 1950 and 1965 the total flow of capital on investment account from the United States to the rest of the world was $23.9 billion, while the corresponding capital inflow from profits was $37.0 billion, for a net inflow into the United States of $13.1 billion. Of this total, $14.9 billion flowed from the United States to Europe and Canada while $11.4 billion flowed in the opposite direction, for a net outflow from the United States of $3.5 billion. Yet, between the United States and all other countries, that is mainly the poor, underdeveloped ones, the situation is reversed: $9.0 billion of investment flowed to these countries while $25.6 billion profit capital flowed out of them, for a net inflow from the poor to the rich of $16.6 billion.

Other available statistics show exactly the same pattern of net capital flow from the underdeveloped countries to the developed ones. The only trouble with these data is that they very much understate the actual flow of capital from the poor underdeveloped countries to the rich developed ones. First of all, they understate the capital flow from the poor to the rich on investment account. Secondly, they obscure the fact that the largest part of the capital which the developed countries own in the underdeveloped ones was never sent from the former to the latter at all but was, on the contrary, acquired by the developed countries in the now underdeveloped ones.

Thus, according to the United States Department of Commerce, of the total capital obtained and employed from all sources by United States operations in Brazil in 1957, 26 per cent came from the United States and the remainder was raised in Brazil, including 36 per cent from Brazilian firms outside the American firms. . . .

Thirdly, these data take account neither of the well-known decline in the underdeveloped countries' relative participation in world trade, nor of the deterioration of the terms of trade which is currently costing the underdeveloped countries far more capital than their net or gross receipts of investments and loans from developed ones. . . .

Fourthly, these data on the flow of investment capital leave out of account the still larger flows of capital from the under-developed countries to the developed ones on other service accounts. In 1962 Latin America spent fully 61 per cent of its foreign exchange earnings on services that were supposedly rendered to it by the developed countries. Half of this, or 30 per cent of the total, was accounted for by officially registered profit remittances and debt service. The other half was composed of Latin American payments to the developed countries, which means mostly the United States, for transportation and insurance, travel, other services, donations, transfer of funds, and errors and omissions (in registered capital flows). . . . Other kinds of capital loss by the underdeveloped countries are not included in these calculations, such as the notorious brain drain, or outflow of human capital that was financed by the poor countries for the subsequent benefit of the rich. Who, we may ask, is diffusing capital to whom?

(A. Gunder Frank, *Latin America: Underdevelopment or Revolution*, Monthly Review Press, 1970, pp. 49–51)

Reading 2   'Megacities' of the twenty-first century

A million new inhabitants will arrive on our planet every four to five days by the year 2000. In terms of sheer numbers the population then will be growing faster than it is today, with 100 million people added each year compared with 77 million in 1975. These figures are revealed by the UN.

The implications of such enormous population growth will be felt not only in the region in which it takes place but in all countries. According to Alexander King of the International Federation of Institutes of Advanced Studies, the immediate problem will be to ensure supplies of food and other essentials to the new arrivals, whose aggregate will be greater than the total world population at the beginning of the 20th century.

Population issues are thus intimately related to other aspects of development – such as land availability, water resources, energy forecasts, upgrading of human resources, and levels of technology. King suggests two approaches: first to assess the global situation as to availability and sustainability of resources and preservation of the environment; second, for each country to determine its population policy concerning material constraints; agricultural, industrial, and other development prospects; and social and cultural ambitions.

A related issue that will need to be considered is growing urbanization. At the beginning of this century there was only one city in the world with five million inhabitants. By the middle of the century, the number rose to ten, and now it is twenty-six. UN experts estimate that by the turn of the century the number will be fifty-five.

Among them, twenty-two will be megacities, each having more than ten million inhabitants.

(B. S. Padmanabhan, *The Hindu*, Madras, 17 Feb. 1985)

Questions

1 What social consequences would you predict from the expected rise in the proportion of people living in a densely populated urban environment?
2 The population explosion, if unchecked, will doom the human race to extinction. Discuss.

Reading 3　Africa's growing food gap

. . . developing countries – which until 1974 were net exporters
of food – have become increasingly dependent upon food
imports. Between 1975 and 1979, they were importing 8 per
cent of their cereal requirements. By the year 2000, if past
trends continue, they will be importing 17 per cent, and in the
case of Africa, no less than 44 per cent. A number of developing countries will undoubtedly run into difficulties in paying
for a rising level of food imports. . . .

In no less than 70 developing countries, the growth
of food production between 1969 and 1971 and 1980 fell
behind the growth of population. It kept ahead or level in
only 56. Africa saw a gradual decline in per capita food production, which was 11 per cent lower in 1980 than a decade
earlier. . . .

If food was equally distributed, the world, and developing
countries as a whole, would have enough food to meet
everyone's needs. But unequal distribution means that malnutrition persists in the midst of plenty in countries with
adequate average calorie intakes as well as those with inadequate averages. It is found predominantly among families who
lack the cash income to buy, or the land and inputs to grow,
enough food for their needs: low-income city dwellers, landless
labourers and smallholders.

(P. Harrison and J. Rowley, 'Human Numbers, Human
Needs', International Planned Parenthood Federation, 1984,
pp 23–4)

(See also Figure 10.1.)

Questions

1　Malthus' predictions about the population of Britain appear not
to have come to pass. They may, however, be said to apply
to some nations in the Third World. Discuss.
2　Third World demographic problems are essentially caused by
disproportionate distribution of economic resources. How far
do you agree with this statement?

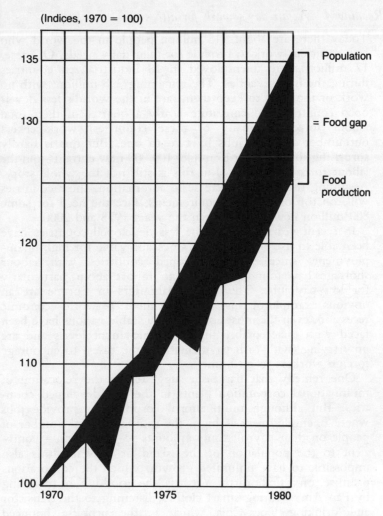

(Indices, 1970 = 100)

Source: 'Human Numbers, Human Needs,' P. Harrison, and J. Rowley, IPPF, 1984, p. 23

Figure 10.1   Africa's growing food gap

Reading 4   A fair day's work for all?

Today there are about 315 million people in the world who lack sufficient work to provide for their daily needs. Of these, 17 million were unemployed in 18 industrialized countries during the mid-seventies. The remaining 298 million, with no work or too little to keep them, are in the world's less developed countries and constitute nearly a quarter of their total labour force. In many of these countries, work-seekers outnumber available jobs by two to one. But this is hardly surprising. In India, for example, 100 000 new entrants join the labour force each week. But this is still not the whole story. Assuming there is no decrease in automation, these countries will, on top of existing requirements, face the need for some 800 million new jobs between the years 1978 and 2000.

In recent years many of the less developed countries have been able to use emigration as an escape valve for high unemployment, since some developed countries with labour shortages have found it expedient to import labour, particularly for low-pay jobs. The foreign labourers in Europe are an obvious example of this. But since the 1974 world economic recession, even the most economically stable nations have been faced with unacceptably high unemployment levels and are now trying (with cash payments in some cases) to encourage foreign workers to go home.

One remedy that has been suggested is the relocation of multinational corporation plants in the less developed countries. But although multinational corporations provide jobs where unemployment is high, the estimated total number of people on their payrolls only amounts to 16 million – equivalent to the population of the island of Taiwan. It is also impossible to have unlimited growth, which the corporations promise, on a finite earth. Yet it is 'the good life' of travelling by Pan Am, wearing smart clothes, listening to the transistor and drinking Coca-Cola which is the promise bounced from the billboard hoardings, the radio commercials and the magazines.

If new employment is to be created there must be 'something' with which to work. For half the labour force of the world, who depend on agriculture, that 'something' is land. In the past when the jobless moved, with their families, to find land it could often be had for the asking. As long as land existed employment could be created with very small amounts of capital – enough to buy a few simple farm implements and seed. But now land for settlement has become scarce, or the property of a few, and the acquisition of land is no longer possible without its redistribution.

Projected increase in world labour force 1978–2000

	Millions	% increase over 1978
World	811	45
Asia	509	51
Africa	121	74
Oceania	5	47
Latin America	96	87
North America	30	28
Europe	30	14
USSR	20	15

(E. McGraw, *Population Today*, Kaye & Ward, 1979, pp. 50–1)

Questions

1 Transferring resources from developed nations would provide underdeveloped nations with a foundation for economic growth and, consequently, bring about a decline in unemployment. Discuss.
2 Examine the implications that high levels of permanently unemployed people within the Third World has for any theory of social development you may have studied.

Documentary readings

The theme of this book has been the conflicting approaches to, and interpretations of, the sociology of development. Trying to find a pathway through the mass of competing theoretical strands is not an easy task, and this chapter continues with a number of extracts in which contrasting standpoints are presented. This is in the hope that they may help the reader to crystallise his or her thinking and gain some further insight into a variety of sociological perspectives.

Readings 5 and 6 present differing interpretations of the term 'development' and underline the difficulties encountered in producing a satisfactory definition. In READING 5, Ward and Dubos adopt a positivist stance in their attempt to define, in a quantitative manner, the criteria by which development may be measured. READING 6 is an attempt at definition which adopts the Marxist model, and includes an acknowledgement of the necessity to include a qualitative aspect in determining the degree of development within a nation.

These are followed by readings which represent contrasting views on the nature of the relationships between nations of the developed and the developing world. READING 7 is a statement describing the nature of aid to the developing world as seen from the point of view of the British government. This should be contrasted with Teresa Hayter's account, in READING 8, of international aid as seen during her analysis of the proceedings of the World Bank in the field of international aid finance.

In READING 9, Professor Rostow sets out clearly the underlying motivation for the process of colonisation in which the developed nations gained control over the population and resources of the underdeveloped. This theme is extended by Maddison in READING 10, where the process of British colonialism is described in some detail, and which stresses the gradual movement from direct to indirect control of the colonised society by the colonists.

READINGS 11 AND 12 present differing views on the nature of the relationship between colonised and colonising nations. Walter Rodney gives evidence of natural resources being expropriated from the African continent in order to strengthen the foundation upon which the economy of the developed nations was based. By contrast, John Goldthorpe takes issue with the notion that the developed nations have 'depended upon the products of the poor', and posits that the fundamental problem is that the developing world lacks a competitive edge in world markets to engage effectively in trade with the advanced nations.

Population and its size and rate of change are frequently the subject of much debate within the analysis of development. Is an increasing population the source of poverty in the Third World, or are other factors involved? Are population statistics signals of impending global disaster, or are they merely part of an ideological deception perpetrated by the demographers of the developed nations? In READING 13, Stephen Enke proposes that economic

development in the Third World is being held back by the growth
of population onceeding the capacity for production. READING 14,
an extract from Ray Bush's work in attempting to explain the
famine in Africa, opposes neo-Malthusian arguments and offers
an alternative viewpoint.

The chapter concludes with two readings on gender, a topic
which is frequently overlooked in the debate over development.
READING 15, by Eric McGraw, assesses the contribution made by
women in the Third World and compares this with their social
status. Emily C. Moore, in READING 16, examines the status
of women in relation to the processes of social change, and
asserts that women must, in the future, be granted equal participation in social planning if any meaningful progress is to be
made.

Reading 5   What is a 'developing Country'?

The phrase 'developing country' has nothing to do with levels
of culture or history or contribution to mankind's heritage of
civilization. In the main it simply means a country which has
not yet crossed the threshold to become a modern, highly technological society, with all the advantages and evils this passage entails. The category includes countries of immensely
old and sophisticated civilizations such as India or China –
which between them make up a third of the human race –
long-established literate and urban-oriented societies in
Latin America and some of the most ancient and continu-
ous of all the world's political units – Egypt, for instance, or
Iran.

A fairly arbitrary estimate is often made which fixes at an
annual income of $500 dollars a head the level at which a
country begins to emerge fully from the pre-technological
condition. But 80 per cent of the nations at or below that level
have an annual per capita incomes of less than $250. This figure
gives a better guide to the bleak realities of personal poverty
for citizens and straitened resources for governments in developing lands. Investment to provide for the essential increases
in productivity needed for development is a third lower than
in high-income countries with incomes over $1000 a year. A
third of this investment is not covered by local savings and
must be secured abroad. Tax revenues, another critical source

of funds for investment, welfare and amenities are only just over half the level in developed lands.

(B. Ward, and R. Dubos, *Only One Earth: the Care and Maintenance of a Small Planet*, Penguin Books, 1976, p. 209)

Questions

1 Critically evaluate the view that 'The phrase "developing country" has nothing to do with levels of culture or history'.
2 Suggest reasons why the writers of the above extract tend to equate development with economic growth.

Reading 6   Development – a Marxist view

More often than not, the term 'development' is used in an exclusive economic sense – the justification being that the type of economy is itself an index of other social features. What then is economic development? A society develops economically as its members increase jointly their capacity for dealing with the environment. This capacity for dealing with the environment is dependent on the extent to which they understand the laws of nature (science), on the extent to which they put that understanding into practice by devising tools (technology), and on the manner in which work is organised. Taking a long-term view, it can be said that there has been constant economic development within human society since the origins of man, because man has multiplied enormously his capacity to win a living from nature. The magnitude of man's achievement is best understood by reflecting on the early history of human society and noting the following: first, the progress from crude stone tools to the use of metals; secondly, the changeover from hunting and gathering wild fruit to the domestication of animals and the growing of food crops; and thirdly, the improvement in organisation of work from being an individ-ualistic activity towards being an activity which assumes a social character through the participation of many. . . .

Every continent independently participated in the early epochs of the extension of man's control over his environment – which means in effect that every continent can point to a period of economic development. . . .

Development was universal because the conditions leading

to economic expansion were universal. Everywhere, man was faced with the task of survival by meeting fundamental material needs; and better tools were a consequence of the interplay between human beings and nature as part of the struggle for survival. Of course, human history is not a record of advances and nothing else. There were periods in every part of the world when there were temporary setbacks and actual reduction of the capacity to produce basic necessities and other services for the population. But the overall tendency was towards increased production, and at given points of time the increase in the quantity of goods was associated with a change in the quality or character of society. . . .

Specialisation and division of labour led to more production as well as inequality of distribution. . . . Through careful study, it is possible to comprehend some of the complicated links between changes in the economic base and changes in the rest of the superstructure of society – including the sphere of ideology and social beliefs. . . . it was to be found that the rise of the state and the superior classes led to the practice whereby common subjects prostrated themselves in the presence of monarchs and aristocrats. When this point had been reached, it became clear that the rough equality of the family had given way to a new state of society.

(W. Rodney, *How Europe Underdeveloped Africa*, Bogle-L'Ouverture Publications, 1972, pp. 10–11)

Questions

1 In what sense other than economic can the term 'development' be used? What sociological perspective might this alternative view represent?
2 Briefly explain what the writer means by the phrase 'complicated links between changes in the economic base and changes in the rest of the superstructure of society'.

Reading 7   The nature of development aid

Two-thirds of the world's population live in poverty. Development aid is a practical way for wealthy countries to help poorer countries to:

* give their people a higher standard of living
* make better use of their land and natural resources
* preserve their environment
* improve their health and education services.

It is also about how to get help quickly to people affected by floods, famine, earthquakes or other emergencies.

It is not a matter of 'handouts'. Our aid is targeted on projects, programmes, people. Aid needs to be carefully planned with the country which has asked for it, particularly to ensure that it fits in with its government's development plans and other policies. Everything has to be agreed and then offered on terms that make sense.

We give aid because there is a moral case for doing so: too many nations are suffering from disease, poverty and an uncertain future. We are more fortunate.

But it is also in our own interest to give aid. There are political and commercial reasons why we should do so. Nations now rely upon each other more than ever before.

Britain already has close links through the Commonwealth with countries in Africa and elsewhere. This means that we have a special understanding and knowledge of the problems many developing countries have to face. We try to help them solve their problems – particularly to find their own solutions and put these into action.

How Britain does this is a story worth telling.

('British Aid', Overseas Development Administration and Central Office of Information, April 1987)

Questions

1 Discuss the view that aid is sponsored by the 'moral case for doing so'.
2 Critically examine the view that inequalities between developed and underdeveloped nations rest upon being more or less 'fortunate'.

Reading 8   Does 'aid' really mean 'help'?

Aid has never been an unconditional transfer of financial resources. . . . Aid from the World Bank is not, under an internal Policy Memorandum which has not been published,

available to countries which nationalize foreign-owned assets
without compensation, which fail to repay their debts or in
which there are claims on behalf of foreign investors which the
Bank considers should be settled. Aid is, in general, available
to countries whose internal political arrangements, foreign
policy alignments, treatment of foreign private investment,
debt servicing record, export policies and so on, are considered
desirable, potentially desirable, or at least acceptable, by the
countries or institutions providing aid, and which do not
appear to threaten their interests.

Some of the conditions attached to aid have also been justi-
fied in term of the need to promote economic development in
underdeveloped countries. Supporters of aid argue that
promoting economic development in poor countries is in the
long-term interests of the developed countries. Therefore they
should try to ensure that development occurs.

(Teresa Hayter, *Aid as Imperialism*, Penguin Books, 1971,
pp. 15–16)

Questions

1 Discuss the view that 'promoting economic development in
  poor countries is in the long-term interests of the developed
  countries'.
2 Critically examine the above extract in the light of two different
  sociological perspectives on development.

Reading 9   Development – a 'non-communist' view

Why . . . was not trade conducted without the creation of
colonies? The answer to this fundamental question has two
elements that need to be sharply distinguished; although they
tend to get intermixed in the flow of history.

First, the struggle for trade took place in a framework where
the major powers were postured, by the nature of history, as
competitors. It is no accident that the major wars of the eighteenth century were wars of succession. The nations were
caught up, by historical inheritance, so to speak, in an inherently competitive system of power—not, in the first instance,
economic power, but military and political power. And in part
the wars in the colonies derived from those larger competitive

compulsions; the compulsion not merely to advance a national interest positively, but to advance a national interest negatively by denying a source of power to another nation. The creation of a trade monopoly in a colonial area was one way to do this, once the new areas were discovered or old areas rediscovered.

But there was a second reason, as well, for the application of military power in the colonies; and this second reason relates not to the power structure of Europe, but to the societal condition of the colonial areas themselves. Colonies were often established initially not to execute a major objective of national policy, nor even to exclude a rival economic power, but to fill a vacuum; this is, to organize a traditional society incapable of self-organization (or unwilling to organize itself) for modern import and export activity, including production for export. Normal trade between equals would often have fulfilled the initial motivation of the intruding power, and a large part of its continuing motivation; for the traditional society had nothing but raw materials to export. And normal trade would have been in many cases tidier, more rational, and even, less costly. In the four centuries preceding 1900, however, the native societies of America, Asia, Africa, and the Middle East were, at various stages, structured and motivated neither to do business with Western Europe nor to protect themselves against Western European arms; and so they were taken over and organized.

(W. W. Rostow, *The Stages of Economic Growth: Non-Communist Manifesto*, Cambridge University Press, 1969, pp. 109–10)

Questions

1 'Why', Rostow asks, 'was not trade conducted without the creation of colonies?' Critically evaluate this question in the light of Rostow's declared non-Communist ideological stance.
2 Write a critique of Rostow's views on colonialism outlined in the extract.

Reading 10 A more pragmatic approach to development

British imperialism was more pragmatic than that of other colonial powers. Its motivation was economic, not evangelical.

There was none of the dedicated Christian fanaticism which the Portuguese and Spanish demonstrated in Latin America and less enthusiasm for cultural diffusion than the French (or the Americans) showed in their colonies. For this reason they Westernized India only to a limited degree.

British interests were of several kinds. At first the main purpose was to achieve a monopolistic trading position. Later it was felt that a regime of free trade would make India a major market for British goods and a source of raw materials, but British capitalists who invested in India, or who sold banking or shipping services there, continued effectively to enjoy monopolistic privileges. India also provided interesting and lucrative employment for a sizeable portion of the British upper middle class, and the remittances they sent home made an appreciable contribution to Britain's balance of payments and capacity to save. Finally, control of India was a key element in the world power structure, in terms of geography, logistics and military manpower. The British were not averse to Indian economic development if it increased their markets but refused to help in areas where they felt there was conflict with their own economic interests or political security. Hence, they refused to give protection to the Indian textile industry until its main competitor became Japan rather than Manchester, and they did almost nothing to further technical education. They introduced some British concepts of property, but did not push them too far when they met vested interests.

The main changes which the British made in Indian society were at the top. They replaced the wasteful warlord aristocracy by a bureaucratic-military establishment, carefully designed by utilitarian technocrats, which was very efficient in maintaining law and order. The greater efficiency of government permitted a substantial reduction in the fiscal burden, and a bigger share of the national product was available for landlords, capitalists and the new professional classes. Some of this upper class income was siphoned off to the UK, but the bulk was spent in India. However, the pattern of consumption changed as the new upper class no longer kept harems and palaces, nor did they wear fine muslins and damascened swords. This caused some painful readjustments in the traditional handicraft sector. It seems likely that there was some increase in productive investment which must have been near zero in Moghul India:

government itself carried out productive investment in railways and irrigation and as a result there was a growth in both agricultural and industrial output. The new elite established a Western life-style using the English language and English schools. New towns and urban amenities were created with segregated suburbs and housing for them. Their habits were copied by the new professional elite of lawyers, doctors, teachers, journalists and businessman. Within this group, old caste barriers were eased and social mobility increased.

As far as the mass of the population were concerned, colonial rule brought few significant changes. The British educational effort was very limited. There were no major changes in village society, in the caste system, the position of untouchables, the joint family system, or in production techniques in agriculture.

British impact on economic and social development was, therefore, limited. Total output and population increased substantially but the gain in per capita output was small or negligible.

(A. Maddison, *Class Structure and Economic Growth*, George Allen & Unwin, 1971, pp. 35–6)

Questions

1 'Modernisation theory is based on false assumptions and has served as a justification of the dominance of Western Capitalism over the rest of the World.' Explain and discuss. (AEB, 1984)
2 Suggest reasons why though the total Gross National Product of a nation may increase, the gain per head of population remains 'small or negligible'.

Reading 11 '. . . from him that hath not shall be taken away . . .'

Much of the dynamism of capitalism lay in the way that growth created more opportunities for further growth. Major industries had by-products, they stimulated local raw material usage, they expanded transport and the building industry. . . .
In the words of the professional economists, those were the beneficial 'backward and forward linkages'. Given that the industries using African raw materials were located outside of Africa, then there could be no beneficial backward and forward

linkages inside Africa. After the second world war, Guinea began to export bauxite. In the hands of French and American capitalists, the bauxite became aluminium. In the metropoles, it went into the making of refractory material, electrical conductors, cigarette foil, kitchen utensils, glass, jewel bearings, abrasives, light-weight structures and aircraft. Guinean bauxite stimulated European shipping and North-American hydro-electric power. In Guinea, the colonial bauxite mining left holes in the ground.

With regard to gold, the financial implications in Europe were enormous, and African gold played its part in the development of the monetary system and of industry and agriculture in the metropoles. But, like bauxite and other minerals, gold is an exhaustible resource. Once it is taken out of a country's soil, that is an absolute loss that cannot be replaced. That simple fact is often obscured so long as production continues, as in South Africa; but it is dramatically brought to attention when the minerals actually disappeared during the colonial epoch. For instance, in the south of Tanganyika, the British mined gold as fast as they could from 1933 onwards at a place called Chunya. By 1953, they had gobbled it all up and exported it abroad. By the end of the colonial period, Chunya was one of the most backward spots in the whole of Tanganyika, which was itself known as the poor Cinderella of East Africa. If that was modernisation, and given the price paid in exploitation and oppression, then Africans would have been better off in the bush.

(W. Rodney, *How Europe Underdeveloped Africa*, London: Bogle-L'Ouverture Publications, 1972, pp. 238–9)

Questions

1 'Africans went into colonialism with a hoe and came out with a hoe.' Discuss.
2 Critically evaluate the writer's statements in the light of one alternative theoretical perspective.

Reading 12   Have 'dependency theorists' got it wrong?

If it were really the case that the rich countries depended on the products of the poor countries, for which they paid them an unduly low price, that would indeed be exploitation. The moral case would be clear-cut; and this situation would be remediable. Since most of the poor countries are now politically independent, their governments could simply insist that a proper price was paid, and cut off supplies if it were not.

But it is not like that. The dependence of the rich countries on supplies from the poor is actually very slight. Faced with a threat to cut off supplies, rich countries and their manufacturing firms could many cases find an alternative source of supply, or switch to using some other product, often one produced at home by an industrial process. The poor countries' actual difficulty, indeed, is quite the reverse – and much more intractable. It is that of marketing their goods at all in the rich countries, of securing outlets for their products, and of holding down their prices in highly competitive markets.

Thus to take one particularly important class of goods, the rich countries meet most of their needs for food by trading among themselves. People in an industrial society like Britain eat wheat from Canada, bacon and dairy produce from Denmark and Eire, lamb from New Zealand; they do not live on rice bought at low prices from starving peasants in Asia. Only a few foodstuffs produced in poor countries are consumed in rich; these include sugar, fats, and oils. But cane sugar produced in tropical countries like the West Indies and Mauritius competes with, and is liable to be replaced by, beet sugar produced in Common Market countries. Indeed, as the Pearson Commission pointed out, many of the products of poor countries compete in this way directly with supplies from within rich countries. For example, cotton grown in India and Egypt competes with domestic supplies in the United States.

In some other cases, products which at first sight might be classified as 'non-competing' in fact face indirect competition from rich countries' own products, for which they are highly substitutable. For example, jute and cotton (again) are subject to strong competition from the man-made fibres, the products of an industrial technology, which besides being cheaper may be regarded as superior in many ways to the fibres produced from tropical plants.

Among commodities which do not face competition from rich-country industrial products, the most important are the tropical beverages – tea, coffee, and cocoa. These, however, can hardly be called necessities on whose supply the rich countries depend for their advantage. Moreover, they are rather substitutable for one another, and though consumers' habits are slow to change they may prove to be price-sensitive in the long term. In marketing these products, then, poor countries are competing with one another if not with home growers in the rich countries.

(J. E. Goldthorpe, *The Sociology of the Third World*, Cambridge University Press, 1979, pp. 98–9)

Questions

1 Discuss the view, stated above, that rich countries do not depend upon the products of poor countries.
2 Examine sociological explanations of the persistence of marked inequalities between developed and underdeveloped societies. (AEB, 1985)

Reading 13   Fewer people could mean larger shares for all

. . . it has become common observation that many less developed countries (LDC's) are not doing well in the race between increasing output and increasing consumers. In fact, output of food in many countries has increased less rapidly than has the number of mouths to feed. A typical LDC may have an annual increase in overall gross national product (GNP) of 4.0 percent and an increase in population of 2.5 per cent for an increase in income per head of only 1.5 percent a year.

In most LDC's the birth rate is not falling. Specific-age fertilities may be rising because of reduced pregnancy wastage and better living conditions. Crude annual birth rates at 45 per 1000 of population approach a biological maximum. Death rates are often around 20 per 1000 and are falling slowly. The result is a doubling of population every 30-odd years.

A doubling of population would ordinarily not be burdensome if the stock of capital and the natural resource endowment could double at the same rate. Unfortunately, LDC's cannot usually save enough each year to double their cumulative investments every 30 years. The national endowment of arable land, proven mineral reserves, and usable water cannot increase at all. . . .

High birth rates also result in high child dependency ratios. A country with a birth rate of over 40 per 1000 may have 40 percent of its population under 15 years of age. These children can produce very little, but they do eat and need some clothing: from birth to 15 years children are consumers but not significant producers.

The conclusion for most LDC's, and especially those with limited natural resources, is that the rate of natural increase must be considerably slowed (emigration being seldom possible on sufficient scale). As death rates decline, birth rates must be reduced even more. A necessary and hopefully practical goal would be a reduction of at least 10 points in the crude birth rate in 10 years and of 15 points in 15 years.

(Stephen Enke, 'Raising Per Capita Income through Fewer Births', General Electric – TEMPO Publication 68TMP-9, Santa Barbara, CA., 1968)

Questions

1 Briefly outline Malthus' views on population. How far does Enke's approach reflect the influence of Malthus?
2 Suggest reasons why 'LDC's cannot usually save enough each year to double their cumulative investments'.

Reading 14   Explaining Africa's famine

Overpopulation is seen as another natural cause of famine in Africa. This 'demographic determinism' dates back to the writings of the Reverend Malthus in the eighteenth century, who argued that population increases geometrically while food production only rises arithmetically. It is an argument taken up more recently by, amongst others, The Food and Agriculture Organisation of the United Nations (FAO). This body has recognised that population growth in Africa rose by 3.1% between 1974–84 while food production only rose by 2%. The increase in population gave African farmers 1 million additional mouths to feed every three weeks. It also disrupted rural labour markets and patterns of urban growth as people migrated to find new forms of employment to pay for food to feed their children.

Ironically, high infant mortality, poverty and poor health

services partly account for Africa's high rates of population growth. The level of infant mortality (per 1000 live births) is similar in African countries today to the level which existed in European countries at the end of the nineteenth century. In the UK at that time the rate was over 140, as it was in 1982 in Chad, Mauritania and the Central African Republic. Infant mortality at the beginning of this century in the US was 120 – as it was in the Sudan, the Ivory Coast and India in 1982. Rates of population growth are likely to fall as economic growth reaches Africa's poor, and as African farmers do not live in constant fear of losing their children in minor ailments like diarrhoea, and the host of infectious diseases long since eradicated in the West.

It is not overpopulation which has caused Africa's recent famine. Neither has it been drought or desertification. A more helpful way of understanding the causes of famine in Africa is to examine the relationship between social classes, institutions and market processes of the capitalist system at work in the world economy and in the specific countries where hunger and malnutrition exist daily.

There is now an enormous weight of literature which locates the causes of Africa's food insecurity in the particular way in which that continent was inserted into the world economy. . . . According to this set of views, colonialism disrupted local patterns of food production and labour supply. Although famines occurred in different parts of Africa before European contact, the latter's demand for cash crops, rather than food crops which may have been used for local consumption, disrupted an indigenous relationship of 'hands to work and mouths to feed'. Colonialism altered the pace and nature of local recovery from drought. This was because European demand for the monetisation of local relationships and its use of the most fertile land dislocated local food systems making African countries more prone to famine.

Africa's susceptibility to famine because of a lean year, perhaps because of a drought or pestilence, has continued into the post-independence 'neo-colonial' period. Where merchant companies of the nineteenth century left off, agribusiness has now taken over. Agribusiness is an umbrella term to describe those multinational companies which control the production, processing and distribution of foodstuffs and control associated technology like tractors, fertilisers and seed. Agribusiness has established a food system – an 'international supermarket' – where low-nutritious luxury foodstuffs are grown in poor Third World countries to export to out-of-season European dinner tables.

A total of 25% of all cultivable land in the Third World is now turned over to cash crops for the markets of the industrialised world. While the export of agricultural commodities has been increasing by 17% annually, the Third World's imports have risen by 20%.

(R. Bush, 'Explaining Africa's Famine', *Social Studies Review* Jan. 1987, 4–5)

Questions

1 (a) Explain why there has been a 'population explosion' in underdeveloped countries.
(b) Examine some of the consequences of such a 'population explosion'. (AEB, 1982)
2 Examine the view that inequality within and between nations is both necessary and inevitable.

Reading 15   The role of women in developing countries

The economic contribution made by women in a number of less developed countries is very great and almost always understated. The fact is that in very poor societies women generally do at least 50 per cent of the work connected with agricultural production and processing, as well as taking care of the children, and the housekeeping. They rise earlier and retire later than anyone else in the family, often working 18 hours a day.

But despite this contribution, women generally suffer the worst malnutrition in poor families. Men are given first claim on available food, children second, the mother last. Malnourished mothers give birth to weak and unhealthy infants, and have problems adequately to nurse them. Such infants often die. To replace these dead infants the mothers are compelled to endure further pregnancies: thus constantly pregnant, or nursing, they are unable to take an active part in the outside workforce. This diminishes their occupational and economic status, which, in turn, reinforces the idea that males are superior. Consequently, sons are deemed more desirable than daughters and when daughters are born, another pregnancy frequently follows in an attempt to produce a son. Repeated pregnancy not only increases the family size but exhausts the mother, weakens her health – and so the whole cycle begins again.

(Eric McGraw, *Population Today*, Kaye & Ward, 1979, p. 88)

Questions

1 'Patterns of health and illness can be understood only in the wider context of social and economic systems.' Examine this view. (AEB, 1985)
2 'It's a girl!' 'It's a boy!' To what extent do such gender definitions determine life chances in different societies? (London, 1984)

Reading 16   Population – one woman's view

Throughout human history in virtually all societies, religious, political, economic, cultural and social institutions have developed to promote maximum child-bearing. Until very recently, this was necessary, since high birth rates were essential to counteract high death rates.

If humanity was to survive, mankind could not afford to ask, 'What do women want? What role is best for them?'

Now the reverse situation may be close at hand – at least in some societies. Women's lives may now have to be manipulated in the opposite direction – to discourage fertility – again in the name of the survival of humanity. We may now well ask whether mankind has the time to let women decide what roles they prefer. Cultural imperatives to reproduce may soon be replaced by sanctions against reproduction – once again it is women's lives that are to be engineered to achieve the desired ends.

Resistance to change imposed from above or from outside is common. Women's resistance to a truly basic change in their life style and sources of satisfaction and prestige will be a major hurdle to successful worldwide reduction in fertility. Women have shown by their abortion activity in the past and the present their refusal to be totally manipulated. Often at considerable risk to themselves and their families, millions of women each year say, in effect, 'No matter what the law says, or the church, or the neighbours or even my husband, and no matter how dangerous it may be, I will not have another child – or I will not have a child at this time.' Their willingness to act against a formidable array of sanctions is a fair illustration of their determination at some point, to manage their own destiny.

This interest in managing their own lives bodes both well and ill for the issue of population control in the future. It bodes well if women can be free to make the kinds of choices which will enable them to fulfil satisfying roles in addition to, or instead of, the role of motherhood. Women's desire for self-determination bodes ill if efforts are made to reduce women's child-bearing function and suitable alternatives are not provided. You can't say to half the human population, 'all right, now you've got to stop doing what it has always been your primary function to do,' without suggesting meaningful substitute activities.

(Emily C. Moore, 'Population Problems from a Woman's Perspective', in *Population: a Clash of Prophets*, E. Pohlman, (ed.), Mentor, 1973, pp. 439–40)

Further reading

There are many books available on matters pertaining to development. The list below is intended to guide the reader towards those texts which can provide more detailed information on matters raised in this introductory volume. Obviously with such an abundance of available material many valuable texts have been omitted. Accordingly, this list is not to be seen as exhaustive but to contain works which are both readable and useful to introductory students, and intended to supplement material already mentioned in the text.

A. N. Agarwala and S. P. Singh (eds), *The Economics of Underdevelopment*, Oxford: Oxford University Press, 1963.

P. Bairoch, *The Economic Development of the Third World since 1900*, London: Methuen, 1975.

M. Barratt-Brown, *The Economics of Imperialism*, Harmondsworth: Penguin, 1974.

———, *The Anatomy of Underdevelopment*, Nottingham: Spokesman Books, 1974.

B. Belassa, *The Newly Industrializing Countries in the World Economy*, Oxford: Pergamon, 1981.

H. Bernstein (ed.), *Underdevelopment and Development*, Harmondsworth: Penguin, 1973.

W. Brandt, *North and South; a Programme for Survival*, London: Pan Books, 1981.

———, *Common Crisis: Co-operation for World Recovery*, London: Pan Books, 1983.

K. Buchanan, *Reflections on Education in the Third World*, Nottingham: Spokesman Books, 1975.

C. Cross, *The Fall of the British Empire*, London: Hodder & Stoughton, 1972.

B. Davey, *The Economic Development of India*, Nottingham: Spokesman Books, 1975.

M. Dobb, *Studies in the Development of Capitalism*, London: Routledge & Kegan Paul, 1946.

————, *Economic Growth and the Underdeveloped Countries*, London: Lawrence and Wishart, 1963.

T. Draper, *Abuse of Power: US Foreign Policy from Cuba to Vietnam*, Harmondsworth: Penguin, 1969.

F. Fanon, *The Wretched of the Earth*, Harmondsworth: Penguin, 1967.

A. G. Frank, *Crisis: in the Third World*, London: Heinemann, 1981.

————, *Crisis: in the World Economy*, London: Heinemann, 1981.

————, *Sociology of Development and the Underdevelopment of Sociology*, London: Pluto Press, 1971.

————, *Latin America: Underdevelopment or Revolution*, New York: Monthly Review Press, 1970.

————, *Capitalism and Underdevelopment in Latin America*, New York: Monthly Review Press, 1969.

J. E. Goldthorpe, *The Sociology of the Third World*, Cambridge: Cambridge University Press, 1975.

N. Harris, *Of Bread and Guns: the World Economy in Crisis*, Harmondsworth: Penguin, 1983.

————, *The End of the Third World*, Harmondsworth: Penguin, 1986.

P. Harrison and J. Rowley, *Human Numbers, Human Needs*, London: International Planned Parenthood Federation, 1984.

T. Hayter, *Aid as Imperialism*, Harmondsworth: Penguin, 1971.

————, *The Creation of World Poverty*, London: Pluto Press, 1981.

T. Hayter and C. Watson, *Aid: Rhetoric and Reality*, London: Pluto Press, 1985.

E. Hobsbawm, *Industry and Empire*, Harmondsworth: Penguin, 1969.

A. M. M. Hoogvelt, *The Sociology of Developing Societies*, London: Macmillan, 1983.

I. Illich, 'Outwitting the Developed Countries', in H. Bernstein (ed.), *Undevelopment and Development*, Harmondsworth: Penguin, 1973, pp. 357–68.

R. Jenkins, *Exploitation*, London: Paladin, 1972.

E. McGraw, *Population Today*, London: Kaye & Ward, 1984.

A. Maddison, *Class Structure and Economic Growth*, London: George Allen & Unwin, 1971.

M. Mamdani, *The Myth of Population Control*, New York: Monthly Review Press, 1972.

R. Mason, *Patterns of Dominance*, Oxford: Oxford University Press, 1970.

D. Meadows, *The Limits to Growth*, London: Pan Books, 1974.

G. M. Meier, (ed.), *Leading Issues in Economic Development: Studies in International Poverty*, New York: Oxford University Press, 1970.

G. M. Meier, and D. Seers (eds), *Pioneers in Development*, New York: World Bank/Oxford University Press, 1984.

J. F. Petras, and M. F. Morley, *How Allende Fell*, Nottingham: Spokesman Books, 1975.

A. Pohlmann (ed.), *Population: a Clash of Prophets*. New York: Mentor, 1973.

R. Rhodes, *Imperialism and Underdevelopment: a Reader*, New York: Monthly Review Press.

W. Rodney, *How Europe Underdeveloped Africa*, London: Bogle-L'Ouverture Publications, 1972.

W. W. Rostow, *The Stages of Economic Growth; a Non-Communist Manifesto*, Cambridge: University Press, 1969.

D. Seers, and J. Leonard, (eds), *Development in a Divided World*, Harmondsworth: Penguin, 1970.

W. Shawcross, *The Quality of Mercy*, London: Fontana, 1985.

B. Warren, *Imperialism, Pioneer of Capitalism,*. London: New Left Books, 1980.

D. Wise and T. Ross, *Invisible Government*, New York: Random House, 1965.

Index